130 ⬛M⬛

ALL-ROUND GENIUS

ALL-ROUND GENIUS

THE UNKNOWN STORY OF BRITAIN'S GREATEST SPORTSMAN

Mick Collins

First published in Great Britain
2006 by Aurum Press Limited,
25 Bedford Avenue,
London WC1B 3AT

A catalogue record for this book is available from the British Library.

ISBN 1 84513 137 1

1 3 5 7 9 10 8 6 4 2
2006 2008 2010 2009 2007

Designed in Bembo by Peter Ward
Typeset by SX Composing DTP, Rayleigh, Essex
Printed and bound in Great Britain by MPG Books, Bodmin

This book is printed on paper certified by the Forest Stewardship
Council as coming from a forest that is well-managed according to
strict environmental, social and economic standards.

For Cassy
With Love

CONTENTS

He achieved so much more than so many modern sportsmen, without ever receiving or asking for a fraction of the praise or the attention. It would have been all too easy for him to make more of a name for himself, to seek out a place in the newspapers, but that just wasn't him, you see, just wasn't what he was all about.

Penny Kavanagh, Max Woosnam's daughter

PROLOGUE

A BUTTER KNIFE AND THE FUTURE DICTATOR

Quite what compelled Max Woosnam to throw Charlie Chaplin into a Hollywood swimming pool has never been entirely clear.

As the captain of the British Davis Cup team, he had simply answered an invitation, sensing the prospect of some fun, and found himself in a Californian mansion. It wasn't the sort of place the son of a Liverpudlian churchman visited too often. Chaplin had just become Hollywood's first million dollar a year performer, and his marriage to a sixteen-year-old bride had collapsed a few months before Woosnam arrived in the country.

At a loose end, living a life of luxury but with nobody to share it, Chaplin – a keen tennis fan – invited Woosnam and his team-mates to come and stay with him. It could have been the perfect friendship – Chaplin, the film star, and Woosnam, champion of Wimbledon and the Olympics, a famous footballer and English hero.

Somehow, unfortunately, the chemistry failed. Chaplin

had grown used to getting his own way. Playing some social tennis with Woosnam would have been fine, but Chaplin wanted to be the star of the show on court every bit as much as he was on screen, a point Woosnam failed to grasp.

Woosnam was supposed to flatter Chaplin, allow him to win the odd point, and make the entire game look far closer and tighter than it actually was. Blatantly not playing seriously, toying with his host, and then upping his game to beat Chaplin with scarcely disguised ease, was not part of the script.

Things went from bad to worse when they decided to move on to a friendly game of table tennis. Woosnam decided the great star of the silent screen needed cheering up, and he had a party piece that never failed to raise a smile.

Woosnam prepared to serve. Shortly before doing so, however, he stepped back, strolled over to a side table, and swapped his bat for a butter knife. Chaplin stared on, prepared to go along with the joke, but intending to end it once the ball had been sent hissing back past Woosnam's swishing cutlery a few times.

Sometime before the great all-rounder finished the game, victorious and mirthful, it dawned on him that perhaps he had tried his host's patience yet again. For Chaplin, being beaten on the tennis court was one thing, but being beaten at table tennis by a man playing with a butter knife in place of a bat was altogether more humbling. As Woosnam chuckled away with the rest of the guests, bemused at what might have caused his host to suffer such a loss of humour, the actor's mood grew ever darker. As Penny Kavanagh, Woosnam's daughter, explains:

> I remember my father talking about Chaplin, and playing tennis and table tennis with him out in Hollywood. Rather sadly, he always said what a dour and miserable man Chaplin was, and how he was never sure that he enjoyed life as much as he might like people to think he did.
>
> My father was truly larger than life, and for an Englishman he was very witty. Terribly good fun to be around, very sharp, and always up for a challenge. If you couldn't keep up, you got left behind, because there was too much going on in life to start dawdling around.

Having regained some semblance of good humour, Chaplin gamely attempted to conceal his annoyance, addressing his guests, drink in hand and casually dressed, putting on a performance. Woosnam, meanwhile, thought the afternoon was going a little flat. How much happier their host would be if it could all end in laughter! And he knew just how to get the laughs going . . .

Walking slowly round to stand behind his host, Woosnam then pounced forwards at the unsuspecting figure in front of him, reached down, grasped Chaplin around the knees, and lifted him up before depositing him forwards, mid-speech, head first into the swimming pool. As the tennis players collapsed with laughter, Chaplin surfaced and stormed off into the house, refusing to emerge until the guests had left the premises.

That Woosnam was playing tricks to liven up the party generated little surprise among his colleagues. There was no disputing that he was exhausting to be around. He flew through life like a spinning top knocking over toy soldiers, doing it all with a grin and a cheery word. People didn't generally get annoyed with him, though − he was never in one place long enough to be irritating, and he never sought a single word of the praise and admiration he generated. Everyone agreed that he was a one-off.

He bustled everywhere, never pausing for breath or a moment's doubt, carrying everyone along on the wake of his enthusiasm. He stood a shade over six feet tall, with the build of a light-heavyweight boxer, and his blond hair generally started the day neatly in place and spent every subsequent minute trying to restyle itself in a more random fashion. The amateur hero of his day, he was a swashbuckling, cigarette-smoking icon, who understood there was more to life than sport, while exceeding the achievements of men who dedicated their whole lives to it. Life for Woosnam was a balance of majesty and modesty. He charmed as he conquered, and never quite understood those who behaved differently.

He lived a Roy of the Rovers life, a vivid Technicolor existence spread across a host of different sports, and never received a penny for his feats, remaining an amateur to the end of his career. Before that career even properly commenced, he had survived four long and brutal years in the trenches, landed at Gallipoli, and commanded men alongside Siegfried Sassoon.

Woosnam's name has largely been forgotten today, his modesty when alive helping to ensure his anonymity when dead. Yet he was an extraordinary character – the never-to-be forgotten sporting hero who somehow slipped into obscurity.

CHAPTER ONE

THE FLEDGLING

For all the excitement he would go on to inspire, the world into which Max Woosnam was born, in Liverpool, on 6 September 1892, was a repressed one. Queen Victoria was in her fifty-fifth year on the throne, and Gladstone, who had just commenced his fourth term as prime minister, was preparing one final, fated attempt to force through his Home Rule Bill.

It was not an age in which to be a maverick, and Woosnam's early influences seemed unlikely to encourage such a development. At first glance, his background offered few clues of what was to come. His father, Charles Maxwell Woosnam, was the canon of the parish of Aberhafesp, a tiny village just outside Newtown in north-west Wales. He acted as Chaplain to the Forces during the years 1912–18, serving with the Monmouthshire Yeomanry during the First World War, and some years earlier served as chaplain to the Tyneside Seaman's Mission.

On the face of it Woosnam senior was a proper and dour sort of man, but the façade was deceptive. Ebullient and charismatic, he was a churchman who left a mark wherever he went. He met his future wife, Mary, while stationed on Tyneside as the chaplain to the Seaman's Mission. When they discovered that they lived on opposite sides of the Tyne to each other, Charles promptly solved the problem by undertaking to stride out, on a regular basis, into the freezing, murky waters and swim powerfully across to his prospective bride. As the people of Tyneside will attest, in certain conditions this is almost as incredible a feat as walking on water. He may have offered guidance and counsel to those who took on the treacherous depths in their boats, but if a quick burst of front crawl was all it took to continue his courtship, then so be it.

He viewed his ministry as an opportunity to celebrate the Lord on a daily basis, in whichever style offered itself to him at that particular moment. For all the Church's sermons and hymns, prayers and psalms, Charles Maxwell Woosnam also knew the value of a gesture, and the importance of displaying his faith as something living and real, not bookish and meek. In an age of Victorian reserve and gentility, Canon Woosnam was a showman, a muscular Christian, and someone to be admired.

Maxwell Woosnam then, even before he began writing his own footnotes in the history books, came from a family with a pedigree for ensuring they were remembered. His father was one of eight children, his grandfather one of four, and his great-grandfather, Bowen Woosnam, the youngest of seven. Even without their evident exuberance, it is easy to see how their name came to be so familiar around the area in which they lived. Sheer weight of numbers ensured that everyone knew a Woosnam, and sheer zest for life ensured nobody forgot them once they did.

It was not only from his father's side that the young Max Woosnam gained his love of life. Mary, his mother, was not keen to slide into the shadows and accept the subdued role so familiar among women of the time. She was an enthusiastic tennis player, and enjoyed playing with her family on the court in the rectory garden at Aberhafesp. As a clergyman's wife she caused something of a stir enjoying an activity which was, at the time, considered most inappropriate.

With one eye on her son's future, it was unsurprising that she took her sport quite so seriously. She became one of the first women to use the backhand stroke, which had been thought of as impossibly daring. Her reasoning was that long skirts prevented her from running around the ball to play it on the forehand, and as she wasn't prepared to lose points on such a regular basis, and in so frustrating a manner, she was left with no other option.

Yet it would be wrong to think that the young Max was swayed entirely by the athleticism of either of his parents. As profound an influence almost certainly came from a slightly more distant and dashing figure. Mary's brother was Hylton 'Punch' Philipson, who kept wicket for England, the Gentlemen, Eton and Oxford. How well the young Max

Woosnam knew his uncle is hard to tell, although in time they would become quite close. Even if he only knew of him by reputation alone, though, it is not hard to imagine that Uncle Hylton would have been something of a role model, if not a hero, to the boy.

On his birth certificate, and by baptism, Philipson was recorded as 'Hilton'. But with an eye on style, and a desire to seem more dashing, by the time he began to achieve sporting fame he had replaced the 'i' with a slightly more swish-sounding 'y'. He was a young boy's dream relative – successful, talented and mysterious in equal parts.

In his third year at Eton, Hylton scored 141 against Max's future school, Winchester, as well as a half-century against Harrow. He subsequently earned his Blue at Oxford in 1887, captaining the side and scoring 150 against Middlesex. Later that year, he played for the Gentlemen at both Lords and the Oval, and toured India with England, travelling to Australia twice and playing a prominent role each time. As *Wisden* recalled of him in his 1936 obituary:

> He was one of the very best wicket-keepers. Standing close to the stumps for most bowlers, he took the ball with easy grace and certainty. While most famous as a cricketer, Punch Philipson held a prominent place in many other games. He earned the title of Racquets Champion at Eton and represented Oxford against Cambridge both at Racquets and in the tennis singles and doubles. He beat

Percy Ashworth for the Racquets Amateur Championship in 1891. C. Wreford-Brown gave him his Association Football Blue as a full back in 1889; so altogether Philipson played for Oxford against Cambridge at four ball games.

A contemporary and racquets partner considered Philipson the best all-rounder he ever knew at Eton.

Philipson may have achieved most of his sporting milestones either shortly before Woosnam was born or within the first few years of his life, but from the moment he was old enough to understand the conversations going on around him, Maxwell Woosnam heard tales of Uncle Hylton and his exploits, competing with distinction as a footballer, tennis player and cricketer. From the earliest age, he saw greatness as being something attainable, rather than remote.

As he grew older and discovered his own sporting talents, no matter how many times people told him to concentrate on just one sport ahead of all others, he knew only too well, having been brought up on tales of his uncle, just how much satisfaction and excitement there was in being an all-rounder.

A more personal account of Woosnam's early years can be found in a piece written by his son, who was also named Max, in 1987. Confused by the way the world had forgotten his father, Max Junior sat down and typed out his memories of the man, filling five yellowing, single-spaced A4 pages in the hope they might one day be used to tell his father's story. It is, in places, a moving and revealing piece of writing, but it is also informative, recording details which would otherwise be impossible to trace:

> My grandfather, who had been such a tireless worker for the Church on Tyneside and in Liverpool, particularly with the Seamen's Mission, had to retire due to ill-health, and took over the Parish at Aberhafesp . . . an area where the Woosnam family had long been, in fact for some centuries, prominent in the Church.
>
> His grandfather and his grandfather's brother had both seen service under General Pottinger in India, one being a Major General and the other a surgeon. They had married sisters from Co. Down, the Misses Bell. It was interesting that my father's sisters, my aunts, later married serving officers in India.
>
> After Canon Woosnam retired, he later bought the hall, whose grounds practically included the church where he would preach and his wife would organise the services and played the old harmonium in an imperial style.

In general, a clergyman's lot was not a lucrative one, and the canon was no exception. It was Mary's family who funded Max's education from prep school through Winchester College to Cambridge. When money was offered, it was readily accepted by his father. Canon Woosnam comes across as a larger-than-life character when one only considers his deeds, but Penny Kavanagh insists that he has been misrepresented by the stories which survive him, and that acts such as swimming across the Tyne were more pragmatic than flamboyant. She offers a more rounded picture:

> My grandfather was an amazing man, he truly was. He was a very quiet man as well, but he was very content to let his actions do the talking. He would sit there at the end of the dining room table, and his wife, my grandmother, who was a huge, strong Northumbrian woman, would sit at the other end as we occupied the middle ground. He was a clever man.

A clever man indeed, and wise enough to be aware of the educational opportunities available to Max with the financial assistance offered by Mary's family, even if it meant taking what would be a heartbreaking decision for most parents today. At the end of the Victorian era, however, those children who were dispatched off to boarding schools were envied, not pitied.

Architecturally at least, with its original buildings designed in a somewhat Tudor manner, Horris Hill School, located just outside Winchester, has a slight air of foreboding. Quite how it must have seemed to Maxwell Woosnam, as he first glanced up at his new home one September morning in 1900, hundreds of miles away from the rest of his family, is anyone's guess. It seems unlikely that it struck him as homely and welcoming. Just short of his eighth birthday, young Max was sent off to be educated as a boarder, returning home every seven or eight weeks. It still seems, to those who never took part in the system, a brutally abrupt way to force a seven-year-old child to grow up.

Today the school is a brighter and livelier place than it was a century ago, and the children who occupy it appear to be happy and content, and certainly free from the fears and strictures which ruled the lives of their predecessors. But a trawl through the school archives highlights starkly how bleak and depressing the life here once was. In 1966 the school launched an appeal to its former pupils, in search of donations and gifts to allow it to continue to develop. The precise amount generated by this request is lost in the mists of time, but it certainly provoked correspondence which vividly illustrates the lasting impression the school made on its alumni.

A fellow schoolmate of Woosnam's, though from the class below him, was one of those who responded to the request. By 1966 he had become an army captain and a respected local councillor – an impressive, persuasive and confident figure perhaps, but the request for a donation dragged up some unwelcome ghosts from the past. He penned a reply:

Dear Sirs,

I am sorry but the miserable memory of the years [approximately 1901 to 1905] which I unhappily spent at

Horris Hill do not make me feel disposed to contribute to
the appeal now being made for it.

. . . In my day there I was seldom happy, usually hungry &
often very cold.

With the exception of Daddy Stow nearly all masters were
intensely disliked.

'Daddy Stow' was the father of Jimmy Stow who, when
the letter requesting donations was sent out, was headmaster
of the school. Whatever happened to the captain during his
time at the school – and quite possibly the continual hardship
of the regime was enough – it plainly affected him deeply.

Although Jimmy Stow reported, in a history of the school
he wrote in 1992, that the appeal was a huge success, and
resulted in sufficient funds for a number of major building
projects to be undertaken, one imagines that the captain was
not alone in having distressing memories of his time at Horris
Hill.

Daddy Snow himself, in his brief memoirs, describes
Woosnam's first-form teacher, Mr Hiddon, in chilling tones:
'He taught the bottom form and ruled it with a rod of iron.
This was not too attractive for the little boys but made the
task of the masters who took the forms just above his vastly
easier.' Given that the general teaching techniques of the day
were hardly liberal, by today's standards, it must have taken a
degree of cruelty to be so fierce to those so young. It does not
require excessive sensitivity to imagine the feelings of a child

in Woosnam's position sent, aged not yet eight, to the other end of the country to board at a school under the gaze of a master known by his own colleagues as having 'ruled with a rod of iron'.

As if life must not have seemed hard enough already, the surroundings in which the pupils resided scarcely offered much by way of respite. Horris Hill is in Hampshire, just three miles from Newbury, Berkshire. There were certain sanitary facilities available to the ratepayers of Berkshire, which did not extend across the border to the school, and in any event, its secluded location left it very isolated.

Alfred Evans, the headmaster and founder of the school, had to make arrangements for heating, water, lighting and drainage, all of which resulted in the most rudimentary of solutions. Water came from springs which were discovered in the rough ground surrounding the north side of the school, and an underground reservoir was eventually built. As a result, until 1912, long after Woosnam had left, taps were located on the ground floor only.

The boys washed in a tiny room, its meagre proportions evidenced by the fact that it eventually became the stationary cupboard, the floor of which was made up of the gravel soil on which the school was built. If a master wanted a wash, jugs of hot and cold water were taken to his room by the staff to fill his hip-bath. Such luxuries as hot water were not, however, available to the pupils, who began each day with a cold bath at 7 a.m.

With no mains gas or electricity, oil lamps provided the lighting on the lower floors, while the dormitories were illuminated by candles. Just to add to the feeling of bleakness, the two classrooms on the north side of the school were built from corrugated iron, while the waste-disposal systems were basic to say the least. The lavatories took the form of earth closets, horrendously cold in the winter, and unbearably foul smelling in the summer. The school, by necessity, was largely self-sufficient and, with the assistance of three gardeners, provided all the fruit and vegetables required to feed its pupils, as well as sheep and pigs kept by the coachman and slaughtered, by Stow's own admission, 'with little care for the rules of hygiene'.

Boys were not allowed home during term time, and even though very occasional visits from parents were permitted, the distance between Horris Hill and Wales would have made it impractical for Canon and Mrs Woosnam to undertake such a trip. Those parents who did come down to visit on a half-term holiday were allowed to take lunch at the school and then 'interview their son on the premises'. As harsh as this sounds, Penny Kavanagh seeks to put it into some form of wider context:

> Sending one's children away to prep school at that age, well, I suppose you could look back now and say that it was cruel, but you have to remember that it was the norm, and that was all there was to it.

You didn't bat against it because everyone else was in the same boat, and in a way it was a much easier world to live in because everyone knew their boundaries, so you didn't cross them if you thought you were going to be smacked or beaten . . . You made a mistake, got punished, remembered not to make it again, and got on with things. I think personally that it made for a very much better nation. If there was a war today, I think a lot of men and boys would find it very much harder even than they did years ago, because they've never really experienced any sort of hardship. They think they have, but they haven't.

Whether a nation's readiness for war is the thermometer by which we check its health is perhaps a moot point, but Penny Kavanagh's views are not uncommon among those of her age and background. In addition, there is no doubt that many former boarders go on to send their own offspring through a similar educational system. Thankfully, these days no establishments host a regime as harsh as Max Woosnam had to endure.

A typical day's schooling was unremitting. Having recovered from their morning bath, pupils attended early school, which consisted of Latin and Greek studies, from quarter past seven until eight o'clock, at which point the boys broke for prayers and breakfast, in that order. School recommenced with further classical studies from nine o'clock until quarter past eleven, and after a further hour's break spent on the field playing traditional Horris Hill games, all of which seem to be interpretations of Bulldog, or something similar, the last class before lunch ran from quarter past twelve to one o'clock.

The afternoon would be largely given over to sporting pursuits, before two more hours of lessons commenced at four o'clock. Tea was served at this point, and the day concluded with an hour of prep between seven and eight o'clock. An average day consisted of three hours of Latin and Greek, an hour of mathematics and a further hour and three-quarters of French, History and Geography. During break time, nobody was allowed inside the school buildings, regardless of the weather, and the masters joined in the games 'with vigour'.

On a Sunday the schedule was, if anything, bleaker. After breakfast the pupils dressed in top hats and Eton suits, carrying umbrellas if it was raining, and walked to the local church for morning service. After church they took another walk before returning to school for half an hour's letter writing and catechism study. They were then allowed lunch and a short break, before walking back to Newtown Church for the four o'clock afternoon service.

Evans was a firm believer that the boys profited from as few distractions (meaning visits or entertainment) as possible, as they stopped them concentrating on work and sport. No ball games were allowed in their free time, and if the sun shone they were allowed to sit on the field, but never to run.

As Geoffrey Bolton, a master who taught at Horris Hill some fifteen years later, recalled, 'the production of a cricket ball would have involved six of the best'. Once a month the teaching staff would depart for a day's golf, leaving Hiddon to remain behind and supervise the pupils. He did this by arranging four games of football, on adjoining pitches arranged in a rectangle, and refereeing them simultaneously. Stow sees this as a 'tribute to the standards of discipline at the school'.

The boys moved up through the school each term depending on their academic performance, rather than their age. As a result, within three years of starting at the school, Woosnam's class contained not a single boy who had been alongside him for that doubtless traumatic first term.

His first promotion found him under the tutelage of Mr Ingram, whom Stow remembers as 'coming from Westminster and Oxford, where he got a Blue for soccer. He was a good teacher, if not very inspiring, and a good player (for those days) of tennis and bridge.' Alongside the stories of Uncle Hylton, Ingram was the second serious all-round sportsman Woosnam had encountered in his young life, and it is easy to imagine the effect this might have had on a sporting and talented child keen to impress in a strange environment.

From Ingram, he moved under the gaze of Mr Haviland, the senior master – 'a most independent character and one who was a little difficult to know at first'. From there it was

Stow himself, and finally on to Evans, the headmaster. Admittedly there weren't many gentle and considerate characters there, but Woosnam still seems to have managed, during the course of his prep-school life, to have picked his way through the toughest of the bunch.

The boys were expected to memorise ferocious amounts of detail and achieve the highest academic standards. E.R. Morgan, who went on to become Bishop of Truro, attended the school at the same time as Woosnam and kept a scrapbook of exams he took while there. A typical mathematics paper of 1902 might have asked Form 7 boys to 'convert 3,724,610 seconds into weeks', while the Latin paper required the translation of the sentence 'I have heard that Numa, a very wise king, ruled the Romans very well.' A geography examination asked him to list all the 'towns, capes etc. which would be passed by a ship sailing from New York to Buenos Aires', and the third-year history exam asks 'What were Scutage, Compurgation, Statute of Labourers, Danegeld, Liveries, Interdict, Witanagemot, Constitutions of Clarendon?' The whole school had to sit the Bible paper, and success merely required the eight- to eleven-year-olds to specify the event linking 'Mahanain, Ziklag, Hebron, Jabesh-Gilead, Engedi and Keilah'. Tending to the spiritual requirements of the people of Truro must have seemed rather tame, in comparison.

In case he might be accused of allowing a moment of idleness to slip into the timetable, Evans kept up the pace right to the very end, as Stow remembers: 'He was always very keen that work should go on until the last possible moment in any term.'

For the first two years of his time there, young Max had the company of his older brother, Charles, to help brighten his days, but by September 1902, Charles had moved up to Winchester College, the famous public school located some thirty miles away. Charles was himself a talented sportsman, and had represented Horris Hill on the cricket field with distinction. In 1902, the cricket XI went through the entire season unbeaten, winning all seven of their contests with Charles batting at number three. A cricket scorebook found in the school's archives offers an extraordinary insight into even the most minor details of the games played, umpired and watched by people who walked Horris Hill's corridors a century ago.

The dates and details, when viewed with hindsight, provide glimpses of historical ironies, destined never to become apparent until years later. On 4 June 1902, for example, Charles Woosnam was left cursing his luck, having been run out for just two, in his first game for Horris Hill against West Downs. On the same day, in Gellingaer, Glamorganshire, five miners were losing their lives after an accident down the pit. As harsh as life could be at Horris Hill, history and hindsight's wider viewpoint remind us that, even with the hardships, its students were the lucky rather than the unlucky few.

It is easy to be moved when glancing through the reports of Woosnam and his contemporaries, if only because we now know of the horrors they were all to experience over the course of the next fifteen years. By the time the First World War arrived, they would be in their early twenties, and would almost without exception find themselves in the line of fire. All those years of cold baths and classics, obedience and discipline, so that they might better hurl themselves over the top when the whistle blew and the guns fired.

At the start of the September term of 1902, young Max, now on his own and under the careful eye of his new class teacher, Stow, made his competitive cricketing debut. Competing as a ten-year-old against boys who had just entered their teens, Woosnam must have been a precocious talent. Although he lacked a vast physical presence (if anything he was slightly small for his age) and the strictures of school life at the time made it unlikely that any degree of extra care was shown towards younger players, Woosnam took to competitive sport with ease. He topped the batting averages in his first season, playing against much older boys, and even picked up a couple of wickets with bowling described as 'tight and careful' – more than his brother Charles had managed in his day. He must have been a particularly frustrating younger sibling at times, if only for his habit of stealing his older brother's sporting glory.

By the following season, however, he was really begin-ning to bloom as a cricketer of some potential. It is all too easy, when provided with a wealth of statistical information such as is retained by Horris Hill, to over-analyse the progress of the season and forget that the boys in question were still just that – boys, albeit boys who had their games particularly well chronicled.

Despite that, he was clearly an exceptional player. Regardless of the standard of the cricket on offer, a privately funded boarding-school team was likely to produce players as good as anywhere in the country, if only on account of the facilities available. Within that system, Woosnam shone.

Two years running Woosnam recorded the highest scores, 92 and 71, and the best averages by far, an influence at the school not seen again until the side was captained by a young lad named Douglas Jardine. Whether by accident or design, the cricketers of Horris Hill seem, with varying degrees of flamboyance, to have had a habit of moving on to cause something of a stir in the wider world.

Woosnam and Jardine certainly shared certain traits beyond their earliest boarding school – both went on from Horris Hill to Winchester, were excellent cricketers and confirmed amateurs, and both travelled abroad to compete on the international sporting stage. There, however, it seems safe to say the similarities end. Woosnam is remembered by those who knew him as much for his cheery disposition as for his physical prowess. 'A friend to all he met', he had, as friends would go on to describe, the knack of 'getting on with people'.

Jardine, in sharp contrast, mastered the art, before refining it on an almost daily basis, of rubbing people up the wrong way – particularly those of Antipodean descent. A talented batsman, he was listed as a Wisden Cricketer of the Year in 1928, and went on to tour Australia. In the first Test he was roundly abused by the crowd on account of his Oxford Harlequin cap, which he insisted on wearing on the field. When an Australian player, Hunter Hendry, sympathised with Jardine for the reception he was receiving, Jardine expressed a lack of surprise, on the grounds that 'all Australians are uneducated and an unruly mob'.

In the next Test, a fellow Englishman, Patsy Hendren, reflected, 'They don't seem to like you very much over here, Mr Jardine,' only to receive the considered reply, 'It's mutual.' By the time England next toured Australia, in 1932–33, the great Don Bradman had come to the fore as the world's finest batsman, while Jardine, presumably on account of his great tact and diplomacy, was named England captain.

He built his side around two fast bowlers, Bill Voce and Harold Larwood, and instigated a tactic he christened 'fast leg theory' and the rest of the world called 'Bodyline'. The ball was pitched short, fast and directly at the batsman, with most of the field waiting on the legside. If connection was made between bat and ball, a fielder waited for the catch. If the batsman missed, and connection was made between him and ball, hospital generally waited for the victim. On the sea journey over, Jardine instructed his side to refer to Bradman

19

as 'the little bastard', and when Australian captain Bill Woodfull was struck and badly injured, Jardine responded with a loud call of 'Well bowled, Harold!' to Larwood. By the final Test, the atmosphere was poisonous. When Jardine swiped away at a fly, bothering him in the outfield, a voice from the crowd called out, 'Leave it alone Jardine, it's the only friend you've got out here.' He brought back the Ashes, and shortly afterwards retired from cricket. He despised Australians, and made the English chattering classes reassess exactly how far they were prepared for a man to go in order to secure victory on their behalf. Australian cricket commentator Alan McGilvray described him as 'the most notorious Englishman since Jack the Ripper'. If Horris Hill thought they had uncovered a cricketing one-off in the shape of Woosnam, Jardine, for a variety of reasons, most of them non-sporting, forced a swift and slightly uncomfortable reconsideration.

While Jardine was causing havoc down under, the school was enjoying only its second unbeaten cricket season since Jardine left, under the captaincy of a boy called Tony Pawson. In a neat piece of symmetry, Pawson again went on to achieve extraordinary things, scoring 237 in his first game at Lords for an U16 Public Schools Combined side, which was, at the time, the highest score by far for an under-18 player at 'Headquarters'.

Both Pawson and his father captained Oxford to innings victories against Cambridge, and he went on to be mentioned

in dispatches for acts of bravery in the Second World War, while serving with the 6th Armoured Division of the Rifle Brigade. He also played football for Charlton Athletic and Oxford University, as well as first-class cricket for Kent, before working as a journalist, and collecting an O.B.E. for his services to fly fishing.

Whatever it was they did to their cricketers at Horris Hill, every now and again one seems to have emerged who achieved quite fantastic things. Woosnam may not have shared, after more careful consideration, all that much with Jardine, but he and Pawson seem a far better match, not least as a result of Pawson's achievements on the football field. Woosnam was plainly a tremendously talented cricketer, and each summer afforded him the opportunity to shine on the sports pitches of the school, but his moments of glory were not limited to the summer months.

Among the copious records at Horris Hill is a yellowing journal written in neat, copperplate handwriting by Mr Lodge, detailing each and every football match Woosnam played during his time at the school. Lodge had been an international footballer himself, and evidently admired Woosnam as a player, while in the spirit of the times, masking any sign of affection for his charge. Leafing through the book, it is possible to glean the first hints of how Woosnam the footballer might develop.

Officially, the Horris Hill football season ran through the term lasting from early September to late December, and no further. In other schools the spring term which followed was set aside for playing rugby, but Horris Hill, like Winchester College, had never taken to the game. The founder of the school, Mr Evans, was a Winchester old boy – a Wykehamist – and the prejudice he developed against rugby as a pupil was carried into the school he opened as a teacher.

The same stubborn sense of officialdom meant that, despite leading the side in ten of the eleven matches, Woosnam is not recorded as captain of the side, on account of not having fulfilled the role in the first game. Had he done so, he would have achieved the double of leading both the cricket and football teams through unbeaten seasons, his versatility already evident at this tender age.

As with the cricket scorebook, many of those who feature in Mr Lodge's journal will have lost their lives on the battlefields of the First World War. His verdicts – 'Philipson was lazy and stupid', and 'Pitman serves no purpose to the team whatsoever' – must have felt desperately final and cutting at the time, but in all likelihood they would be rendered painfully poignant, a little over a decade later, when 'charging forwards towards the opposition' took on a more chilling meaning.

By his final year at the school, Woosnam had developed into a fine player, for his age, by any standards. Lodge must have realised this as he recorded how it was usually one talented young man leading his side to win after win: 'A good passer like Woosnam is simply good because he looks about him and takes in at a glance a plan of the surrounding players. When the opening is found he wastes no time in getting the ball to its proper place, otherwise in a few seconds the chance will have gone.'

Although he ended his cricketing endeavours at the school with a win, Woosnam, was forced to settle for a draw in his last outing in their football colours. As Lodge makes clear though, in a style adopted by thousands of managers ever since, they deserved more than just a point from the match: 'Woosnam was on his absolute best form, and had some desperate bad luck with his shots. At times, in front of goal, an ounce of dash and vigour is worth a ton of science.'

Woosnam emerged from the school with an extra-ordinary energy and enthusiasm for life, and a sense of discipline to run alongside the dreams and ambitions that Hylton's achievements had instilled in him. It may have broken many less confident and physically boisterous boys, but Horris Hill, even with its pseudo-militaristic early twentieth-century ways, played a huge part in turning Max Woosnam into the man he was to become.

Leaving Horris Hill for the last time in 1905, Woosnam returned home to the vicarage at Aberhafesp for the Christmas holidays, possibly even travelling with his older brother. When he journeyed back a few weeks later, he would be twenty miles further down the road, joining Charles at Winchester on a permanent basis.

Woosnam arrived at Winchester with his brother in the spring term 1906. Their closeness, the foundations for which had doubtless been strengthened by their shared experiences at Horris Hill, was further enhanced when Max was placed, alongside Charles, into Hawkins' House, known to all as Chawker's House after the surname of the original housemaster.

A five-minute stroll from the main entrance to the school, past St Michael's Church, Chawker's feels much as it must have done a century ago. Essentially a large, detached house, with a gravelled drive along the side of a large lawn, it retains a sense of otherworldliness. On the walls surrounding the dining room, are pictures of Chawker's finest sporting teams of years gone past, including several featuring Woosnam, while dark wooden inscribed panels record the achievements of its inhabitants down the years.

Along the walls of the quad in the main school are memorials and plaques marking the achievements and resting places of many famous Wykehamists. In a far corner is a white and grey stone collage marking the life of George Mallory, the mountaineer who, in the words of the inscription beneath the beautiful stone image, 'was lost to human sight between heaven and earth while attempting to reach the summit of Everest, 8 June 1924'.

While Mallory challenged the boundaries of human endurance, other former Wykehamists of Woosnam's era found that fame would come from challenging the authorities. When Woosnam was entering his fourth year, a young boy called Oswald Mosley arrived, listening intently as his teachers prepared him for the challenges the outside world would one day throw his way. Nobody could have anticipated that this wide-eyed and expectant pupil would go on to be a socialite, fascist, and friend to Joseph Goebbels and Adolf Hitler. The single-mindedness their education helped to foster, while driving Woosnam to greater things, could, as Mosley and, to a lesser extent, Jardine demonstrated, be a dangerous character trait.

Woosnam's first housemaster was Edward Buckland, whose own sporting pedigree was further influential. Buckland, like virtually all Woosnam's teachers, was Oxbridge educated, having played in the cricket XI for four years with some distinction. Upon leaving university, he had played for Hampshire and Middlesex, leaving, like so many of the characters Woosnam appears to have met through his life, an intriguing legacy, thanks in no small part to his bowling styles, described as 'right arm off-break, and right arm fast-underarm'. Eccentric by today's standards, but far from unusual back in the late nineteenth century.

In Buckland, Woosnam seemed to have found the perfect figure to keep a watchful eye over his sporting talents, but it was not to be. Just a month after they met, illness prematurely claimed Buckland's life, and Woosnam found himself attending his housemaster's funeral. Despite this upset, Woosnam appears to have soon settled in to Winchester life and, owing to his talents, began playing alongside boys considerably older than him from his very first term.

He was selected for the House XI within his first half term at Winchester, and claimed the only goal of the inter-house final in the first minute of the match. A picture, hanging high on the refectory wall on Chawker's House, shows the victorious team sitting in familiar formation, complete with mascot and large, silver trophy on the floor in front of them. On further inspection, however, the figure in the foreground is not a mascot, but a player – Woosnam. A foot or more shorter than the oldest of the boys in the side, a thirteen-year-old playing against eighteen-year-olds; it is a remarkable image.

In the side along with him was Charles, team mate for the first time. Quite how the older Woosnam reacted to his precociously talented younger brother turning up and stealing the glory is not documented, but only a saint would not have heaved the occasional exasperated sigh.

Unfortunately for Charles, the cricket season offered no respite, as the sporting talents of his younger brother were showing no signs of losing momentum. He played for the house cricket team for the whole season, and helped them to win each and every game they played. After two terms playing competitive sport alongside, in effect, grown men, Woosnam, just into his teens, had yet to lose a match and had two trophies to his name.

As Max grew bigger, stronger and better, it might have

been with some relief that the older brother left the school in Easter 1908. In the term before he departed, the two brothers played alongside each other for the school football XI, and Chawker's House won both the Ellis Cup and the Flower Cup (known as the Flower Pot).

Max, meanwhile, was also enjoying great success in Winchester's own version of football, known as winkies. The game was played on a small, narrow pitch known as a canvas, and it featured rules such as 'hotwatches', 'scrums' and 'hots'. It is a mutant game, spawned from a one-night stand between rugby and football, cherished by Wykehamists and unintelligible to outsiders.

Several years ago, the late Peter Cook found himself on holiday in Egypt. By the side of a swimming pool, and looking for amusement, he constructed the game of Abu Simbel, which involved rolling a beach ball around the pool achieving the likes of 'ruffords', 'strottling', 'troats', 'codrons' and 'valiants'; he then spent the afternoon convincing the locals it was a popular English sport. As a satire on winkies and all it represented, it was characteristically brilliant. Regardless of its highly exclusive and virtually meaningless place in the wider world of sport, however, Woosnam's abilities at this strangest of games comes as little surprise.

Two years after Charles left his younger brother and the relative comforts of Chawker's, he suffered a fatal reaction to an injection administered before a posting to India, with the army. Maxwell, aged eighteen, became the only living son, and his sisters Monica and Gaynor, aged twelve and ten respectively – with whom he had been given scant opportunity to spend any real time – mourned a brother they can scarcely have known.

Maxwell had grown into a barrel-chested teenager, with unruly hair and thighs like telephone poles. His physical presence coupled with his ebullient nature and manic bravery must have made him a fearsome sporting opponent for the average schoolboy. Chawker's won the Turner Cup for cricket in 1908, with Woosnam by now a regular member of the side. At the start of the winter term of 1908, he was selected to play golf for the school, a team of which he remained a part for the rest of his time at Winchester.

It comes as little surprise to hear that he played off scratch – with no need of any 'head start' when playing even the very best – and it seems his naturally brilliant hand-eye coordination allowed him to master all but the finest features of the game with very little difficulty. He went on to become a member and eventually president of the school golfing committee, running it with characteristic diligence and flair. He might well have gone on to carve out a highly successful career as a golfer – he was certainly good enough – but the sheer length of time it took to play the game, rather than any difficulties it posed him, dissuaded him. A man could play any other sport half a dozen times over in the time it took to play a couple of rounds of golf and, for Woosnam, time was always something to be carefully rationed.

While sport undoubtedly marked his progress through the school, his achievements off the field perhaps tell us something of how Woosnam the man, rather than just the sportsman, was developing. Just after the Christmas of 1908, almost exactly a year after Charles moved on, Max was made a house prefect, as well as being awarded his soccer cap and house tie. Having entered Winchester's sporting world with dizzying speed, it had perhaps taken him a couple of years to slow down and look around at the wider picture of what the school had to offer him.

Academically, Woosnam never excelled, certainly not by Winchester's high standards. Having achieved an acceptable classroom standard early in his schooling, it seems he spent the best part of three years languishing in the foothills of this academic mountain, never troubling himself to climb much higher. For him, the last three years at Winchester meant managing committees, playing sport and keeping an eye on the good running of Chawker's House, in his role as Senior Commoner. Getting along with people and playing sport were two talents Woosnam would go on to utilise to stunning effect throughout the rest of his life.

Perhaps fittingly, he rounded off his time at Winchester with a sporting triumph, having been named as school cricket captain – 'Captain of Lords', as the college refers to its side. The details are recorded in another leather-bound journal, stored away on a dusty bookshelf and holding the most intricate details of an age gone by. They also record a match he played for the Public Schools XI, against the MCC at Lords. Woosnam went in to bat with the Public Schools struggling terribly at 65 for 5, forged a century partnership, and eventually ran out of partners, having saved the game with his 144 not out. As the game was declared a draw, he was 33 not out in the second innings, having enjoyed his debut at the home of cricket so much, he declined to surrender his wicket at any stage.

Each page of the record book represents a term in the life of Chawker's House, and the entry for Cloister Time 1911 is inscribed in neat, close handwriting, and signed in black ink 'M.Woosnam, Sen: Co: Pre'. Almost a century ago Woosnam sat and wrote out the page, recording the achievements of both himself and his housemates, before signing it, dating it and heading off, purposeful and charismatic, into the next stage of an extraordinary life. In the years which followed, signing autographs would become a far more normal part of his daily routine, but while his achievements had thus far been impressive, they had yet to mean anything of note on a wider stage.

CHAPTER TWO

CAMBRIDGE BLUES

While Winchester had provided Woosnam with a stage for his sporting talents, he had not lost too much sleep worrying about his academic progress. He was in a dangerous position – academically able but instinctively uninterested. In football terms, he was too good to be relegated, yet had no interest in pushing on and trying to win the league, happy to sit in mid-table. Life for Max Woosnam would always be about scorebooks, not textbooks.

It was fitting, perhaps inevitable, that when the time came to leave Winchester he headed off to Trinity College, Cambridge, with its well-established sporting credentials. It is hard to see Woosnam feeling at home in an institution with a reputation for academic excellence alone, or to see such a place particularly interested in having him as a student. At Trinity, his achievements on the playing field were allowed to take precedence over his academic studies.

He arrived there in June 1911, his reputation with bat and ball provoking an invitation to spend the summer playing cricket before his formal enrolment in the autumn. As with Winchester, the fees involved were beyond the financial means of his father, and the costs of his degree in classics were met once again by his mother's family. Without their input, his life would already have been set on a different, more mundane path, but even in their wildest dreams they could not have guessed what a sporting springboard the academic education they bought their young relative would be.

With university still more of a luxury than a right, Woosnam was surrounded by students from the most privileged backgrounds, and his sporting prowess, coupled with his bubbly, affable nature, saw him find swift acceptance. As his sporting career blossomed, this character trait would help make him a hero to the working and the chattering classes alike, and yet it was an approach rooted in pragmatism.

When he arrived at Trinity, people wondered whether the prodigiously talented schoolboy athlete might realise his sporting potential. By the time he left, he had represented his university (earned his Blue) in five separate sports – football, tennis, real tennis, golf and cricket – and gained a reputation which stood up to scrutiny alongside all but the very best sportsmen in the land.

After three years of study he got a rather undistinguished degree pass at Ordinary level, graduating with his BA in absentia on 18 December 1915. He returned to Trinity after the war, principally to play sport, and collected his MA on 14 June 1919. As the Board of Graduate Studies at the university explains: 'The MA degree, which in many universities is awarded by examination, is in Cambridge conferred only on holders of the BA degree of the university and on certain other senior members of the university. It is not available as a postgraduate qualification in the sense in which that term is generally used.'

It was perhaps, then, a good thing that Woosnam had strings to his bow other than of the academic variety. A run-of-the-mill degree and a 'buy one, get one free' MA were, on their own, a less than spectacular return on an investment of four years of education. Yet, it mattered not. Studying at Trinity, with its sporting history, suited Woosnam perfectly, with his academic life becoming slowly ever more of a side show to the main reason for his presence. Had he turned up at his college without books, there might have been a few eyebrows gently raised. Had he turned up without boots and rackets, the consternation would have been considerably more pronounced.

From the small house that he shared with friends at number 14 Portugal Street, it was a short stroll to the university library. Passing along Magdalene Street, before ignoring Jesus Lane and skipping through All Saints Passage and into Trinity Street, was about as close to academia as Max chose to get. Although clad in the requisite cap and gown demanded by the university rules, he usually had sporting equipment tucked under his arm, not books.

He was forced to juggle his various responsibilities in

much the way he had done at Winchester, trying to make time for everything he wanted to do, without allowing his studies to fall completely by the wayside. His experiences of university cricket, where he had shone so brightly at school, provided an early indication of the difficulties of timetabling his all-round talents. The university archives offer evidence of the competing demands on his time, and along the way help to demolish some myths about him which have become accepted as established fact.

The sporting world of the day was divided along amateur and professional lines into Gentlemen and Players. Gentlemen often had private incomes, or substantial family fortunes behind them, and embraced amateurism not necessarily because of some great moral conviction but because they could afford to play their sport unpaid, with nobody to dictate where and when they performed. Players had no such luxury, and existed on a fraction of the money today's top sportsmen would collect. In return they were treated in a slightly second-class fashion, as if they sullied the great amateur ideal by means of their existence.

A glance through the cricket-club scorebook of the day tells an interesting tale, its pages filled with names such as the Honourable A. Windsor-Clive and the Honourable H.G.H. Mullholland, confirming that Woosnam's cricketing team mates were a privileged group, with the financial freedom to live the amateur dream. Woosnam, his education paid for by the well-to-do side of the family, enjoyed no such riches and no such freedom. The lifestyle of a Gentleman was beyond him, but neither did he show any desire to forge a professional career.

Perhaps this attitude was in some way influenced by his family background, with his father's life as a minister and Uncle Hylton's amateur glories, but it led to a decision to back away from a game at which his early promise had been immense. By 1914 he had been twelfth man in the Varsity contest against Oxford, but had otherwise failed to make the impression one might have expected. His son, Max, was firmly of the opinion that it was his father's inability to concentrate on the game as completely as he wanted to which led him to give it up in frustration, but the truth is more straightforward.

In the early months of the 1913 cricket season, as if determined to prove that sport rather than study was all-important to them, the Cambridge side played matches on thirty out of fifty-six days, many of them away fixtures involving overnight trips back to the university. If Woosnam was to play serious cricket, he would have little time left to concentrate on anything else, and limiting himself to any one sport, let alone leaving time for studying, was not an idea which ever appealed to his nature. Woosnam's decision to walk away from the game was made on pragmatic grounds, relating to pressure of time, rather than for any idealistic reasons. Besides, it was never his belief that to embrace amateurism required one to condem professionalism.

If his summers were crowded, however, he could at least concentrate on just one discipline, football, through most of the winter. He represented Cambridge from 1912 to 1914, captaining them in his last season and justifying the predictions made about him over the course of his schooling. His style was bustling and dynamic, as it would remain throughout his footballing career, involving him in the thick of the defensive action and utilising his physical attributes to deliver long passes and win the sort of challenges the game no longer entertains.

He had developed into a powerful man, broad of chest, thickset and with enormous, muscular thighs which sent him bouncing around whichever sporting venue the challenge of the day required. In addition, he had grown a moustache, in the style of the time – something with which he was perhaps slightly ill at ease, varying as it did from pencil-thin to fully grown, and occasionally disappearing altogether only to return again much later in his life.

A cartoon produced in the *Daily Graphic* on 9 February 1914, concerning the Varsity Match, features a large caricature of Woosnam, this time minus the facial hair, with the caption 'Woosnam, the Cambridge skipper, was the best half on the field', while *The Times* describes Woosnam as 'captain courageous'. Of the match, they observed that 'Woosnam's great defensive play came in very useful at this trying period for Cambridge, and Oxford were driven back after a long attack.'

His appearances as a footballer for Cambridge were not documented as fully as one might expect, although he evidently attracted attention from a number of senior professional clubs as a result of his performances. Being captain of the university football team, however, meant that he was well known there throughout the winter months, while his summertime activities ensured that his reputation stretched year round.

His colleagues at Trinity found him engaging and ebullient, while his elders also saw the more modest side of him – the side which would never think himself to be above the next person simply because of his athletic talent. His schedule never allowed him to stay in one place for very long, a cause for wry amusement among his fellow students, as he raced around perpetually searching for a new challenge.

Knowingly or not, millions of people are familiar with a pastiche of sporting life at Trinity a few years after Woosnam was there, courtesy of the film *Chariots of Fire*. Admittedly, artistic licence was stretched in all manner of directions when David Puttnam recreated Harold Abrahams' dash around Trinity's Great Court, traditionally held, with quintessentially English eccentricity, at noon on the day of the Matriculation Dinner – Abrahams never actually attempted the Trinity Great Court run while at Cambridge, so whether he could have traversed its 367 metres in the forty-three seconds it takes the clock to strike twelve we will never know. Despite its slightly flowery view of things, the film paints a pleasing picture of the sort of university life Woosnam might have led.

While his winters were busy, balancing what study he did manage with the demands of playing regular football, it was in the summer that his schedule became genuinely frantic. 'Multi-tasking' may be a new term, but the practice, as Woosnam demonstrated, is not. He spent three years playing for the golf club, a game he had only flirted with occasionally at Winchester, yet was apparently sufficiently competent in to earn his Blue. 'Woosnam drives the ball with great power and accuracy,' commented a report at the time;

> He clears obstacles other players are forced to avoid by more circuitous routes, sending his drives far and high. Were his play around the green as accomplished as his play from the tee, he would doubtless be one of the players of his era. Should he choose to devote himself to the game, for it is one of several he enjoys, this may yet be the case.

He played golf the way he played everything else – indeed, in the manner he lived his life. That Woosnam opted to hit the ball as far as his strength would allow whenever given the chance seems entirely appropriate. Unfortunately for him, no matter how vigorous and expansive his own interpretation of the game of golf, others saw it as a more sedentary affair.

Though played more swiftly than today, rounds still took several hours, and the delays and the waiting around did not sit easily with Woosnam's nature. Much as he enjoyed the game, it couldn't offer him the same excitement and challenge as his beloved football, nor the cut and thrust of his other favoured summer pastimes, as the Cambridge sunshine saw him take the opportunity to reacquaint himself with a game he had enjoyed playing so much in the vicarage gardens at Aberhafesp. With cricket bat or golf club in hand, Woosnam had shown he was a fearsome competitor, but with a tennis racquet he was on a different level altogether.

He earned his tennis blue with characteristic ease, already blessed with an all-round game comfortably superior to that of almost any other university player of the day. Not overly reliant on any one approach, Woosnam simply utilised his general athletic abilities and unerring instinct for the way a sport was best played, to produce a hybrid style almost impossible to match. He was athletic, competitive, dogged and brave, and the prospect of channelling these assets into one single discipline was never, thankfully, one he seriously considered.

More often than not, his participation in any one particular sport came about on a whim, simply because the activity in question just happened to appeal to him at the time. Such were the benefits of amateurism and playing games simply for the sheer thrill and enjoyment of them. Woosnam's inquisitive sporting spirit was always likely to lead him to some unlikely pursuits; the adventure with winkies springs to mind, and prime amongst that particular category were the obscure challenges offered to him by real tennis.

Despite never having played before arriving at Trinity, he became a stalwart of the Cambridge Real Tennis Club, and played for them throughout his time there. Trinity dominated the university's Challenge Cup, awarded annually to the best real tennis team, which the college had won for eleven consecutive years. Newspaper cuttings of the time relating to the game of real tennis at Cambridge offer a fascinating insight into Woosnam's sporting talents, as witnessed by the journalists of the day.

The first mention of him comes in a report in *The Times* dated 29 May 1913 of a game between Cambridge and the Prince's Club of Knightsbridge:

> The Cambridge players included two undergraduates, Mr H.W. Leatham and Mr M. Woosnam. Mr Woosnam, who has only recently started tennis, and has wonderful powers of return, shows the greatest promise.
>
> It is most encouraging to find tennis at Cambridge, one of the most famous homes of the game, in so flourishing a condition. Arthur Twinn, the professional at the courts, took the greatest pains to make the day a success.'

Real tennis was a curious sport by any standards. It held none of the glory of cricket or golf, yet it fitted his timetable and his desire for something active and challenging, and Woosnam was positively attracted by its oddness, rather than put off by it.

Its mystique was added to by what one can only speculate to have been something of an 'arrangement' between the professional who kept the Cambridge courts, and the news-papers who covered the events there. *The Times* ended its report of 10 November 1913, 'Twinn, the professional, worked hard to make the day a success.' Then there was the report in the *Field*, five days later, 'Twinn, the head professional, made excellent arrangements.' And by February of the following year, *The Times* was once more commenting on how 'Arthur Twinn, the Cambridge professional, made excellent arrangements for the programme of matches.' If Arthur Twinn had an agent, whatever he was paying them, it wasn't enough.

As far as Woosnam was concerned, the praise being lavished on him was still, generally speaking, fulsome. There were, however, those who became gradually more frustrated at what they saw as his refusal to concentrate solely on one game. The *Field*'s reporter, originally a staunch fan, slowly found it harder to conceal his concern at what he plainly saw as the sullying of Woosnam's real tennis game with the continual influence of lawn tennis. The need to mention this 'other' form of tennis did little to lighten his mood: 'Woosnam plays a mixture of lawn tennis and racquets in the tennis court . . . Unless he remodels his methods he cannot get very much better than he is at present.' Obviously, in keeping with tradition, the article concludes: 'The arrangements made by Twinn, the professional, could not be faulted in any way.'

The fact that Woosnam won his Blue and, along with Leatham, claimed the Varsity match for Cambridge with relative ease, seems to have meant little to the journalist. It takes the briefest read between the lines to see that the establishment, at least as far as real tennis was concerned, was not impressed by Woosnam's versatility – this fair-haired mass of energy and enthusiasm was failing to make their game look sufficiently difficult.

While his habit of making things look effortless must have grown wearisome from time to time, his fellow sportsmen genuinely seemed to find it difficult to say a bad word about him. Those who criticised him tended to be not competitors but observers, whose opinion he placed much less weight on.

Despite his dalliance with real tennis, the lawn tennis press seemed aware, even at this early stage, that it was their game to which Woosnam was first and most attracted. In the 1914 Varsity match he was unbeaten, and the reporter from *Lawn Tennis and Badminton* commented on his 'grasshopper-like agility', as he dispatched all comers with relative ease, while Cambridge claimed a comprehensive victory.

The calibre of opposition routinely chosen to compete against Woosnam's side was a mark of the strength of varsity tennis at the time, and their successes underline the point still further. By 1919, for example, when he had returned to Trinity after the war, Cambridge played a game against the United States Army, and emerged 9–0 victors, with Woosnam failing to drop a set throughout.

Woosnam had many fans among the ranks of the lawn-tennis press. Sometimes, as this cutting from *Lawn Tennis and*

Badminton demonstrates, this ran to piling huge, and mildly absurd pressures on his shoulders, as well as the occasional and gloriously inaccurate prediction:

> Woosnam is the most promising player Cambridge has thrown up in over a decade. But he is essentially a versatile games-man, a natural athlete, and since the highest form at lawn tennis demands the sternest concentration (you cannot mix your pastimes and win at Wimbledon), he will have to make his choice quickly if he is to go right to the front. Perhaps that is not his ambition. For some things I rather hope it is not; for obsessional specialism in English games has its moral drawbacks in these days of rebuilding.

Despite Cambridge suffering defeat in the 1919 Varsity match, Woosnam's contribution was highly praised, and he continued to fight off the threat of 'obsessional specialism' with customary vigour and enthusiasm.

For many sportsmen, arriving at university meant accepting that after years of being the dominant presence at school, they had finally become smaller fish in a bigger pond. Varsity sport matched them against those physically equipped to match and better them. For many, it must have come as something of a shock.

For Woosnam it came simply as confirmation, if indeed he possessed deep-rooted doubts about his own talents that he was every bit as good as people had suggested, and probably better. He attacked sporting life at Cambridge with the same gusto he had done at Horris Hill and Winchester, and in doing so met with just as much success. Cambridge was the place where Max Woosnam got a real sense of just how good a sportsman he was.

The snide remarks that appeared in the press in relation to his real tennis, and the feeling that he was somehow playing at the game, rather than taking it seriously, would all have opened his eyes a little. Not everyone automatically wanted him to succeed − not everyone welcomed a man who accepted challenges for the sheer joy of doing so, and who investigated his own talent with such naïve delight.

In the years which followed, Max Woosnam would be given many reasons to look back on his schooldays, however hard they may have seemed at the time, and reflect on how lucky he had been to live such a sheltered life. Reality was soon to intrude.

CHAPTER THREE

IF IT'S TUESDAY IT MUST BE BRAZIL

Having been invited to play for the famous and successful amateur side the Corinthians, when in only his second year at Cambridge, it was clear that Woosnam was not just a player of some skill, but that physically he had grown particularly strong and able for his age. While varsity sport was fast and clever, it lacked the physical element demanded by first-class football. That he was thought capable of playing at such a level while still a student, and that he relished the challenge, reflects in equal parts his attitude and his ability.

As with any amateur sportsman of his era, Woosnam's life was one of contrasts. In his case, his exploits and the attention they generated meant that the contrasts were greater than most, but the idea of having two vastly different lives, one based around work, the other around sport, was for the vast majority the norm, rather than the exception. In an era where sporting amateurism was something to aspire to, not settle for, when Woosnam was referred to in newspapers as 'the famous amateur', it was with genuine respect, rather than patronising affection.

The whole concept of professionalism in sport was very much in its infancy, and while the Football League was still slowly expanding into the body we recognise today, the rewards for playing professionally were meagre. Compared to modern professional footballers, the vast majority paid to play in the period after the end of the First World War were on little more than subsistence wages. While it is easy to see Woosnam as some kind of amateur campaigner against this seeming injustice, that would, for the time being, be stretching the truth.

Coming straight after exams at the end of the summer term, in June 1913, the forthcoming tour of Brazil was an exciting prospect for any young footballer. However, despite the importance Brazilian football would go on to have in the sporting world, the Corinthians were making the trip reluctantly, as a result of their staunch beliefs about amateurism.

The Corinthians had been formed in 1882 by N.L. 'Pa' Jackson, a former public schoolboy who sought to achieve two rather different aims. First, and most importantly to him, his side were to promote the ideals of sportsmanship and fair play at every available opportunity. That having been achieved, the Corinthians would, it was hoped, challenge the increasing dominance Scotland enjoyed in British football.

The English persisted in playing a visually pleasing yet hopelessly outdated and ineffective dribbling game, long after the Scots had adopted a passing system which was superior in almost every way. The Scottish team were largely from the Glasgow area, and regularly trained together, while the England players came from all parts of the country, and only met up shortly before matches.

The new club gathered together as many former Oxford and Cambridge players as it could muster, with the sole intention of beating the Scots. It seems ironic that this amateur side, brought together in pursuance of the finest traditions of amateur sportsmanship, was so unashamed of this aim. It made perfect sense to Woosnam, who never had any difficulty combining his belief in playing in the right spirit with a ferocious desire to win. Not being paid for the game didn't mean a lack of concern for the result.

The Corinthians believed that an Englishman should show fairness to all, compete with integrity and even-handedness, and above all should play for the love of the game, not the lure of finance. If he could turn the tables on the Scots along the way, so much the better — losing with dignity and honour was very important, but winning with dignity and honour was more important still. Ultimately, they served as a convenient pool of players, familiar with each other and used to playing together, in order that England's cause might be well served when so required. Their distrust and disquiet with anyone who played their sport on a professional basis bordered at times on the neurotic. It was certainly more than Max Woosnam felt entirely happy with.

Such was their aversion to what they considered the polluting influence of professionalism that they spent the first eighteen years of their existence abiding by a constitution which forbade playing in any competition whatsoever, lest they might come up against someone less fanatically amateur. Their first competitive game eventually saw their first triumph, however, as they defeated the current football league champions, Aston Villa, to lift the Sheriff of London Shield in 1900. In 1902 Real Madrid adopted the Corinthian white strip, and in 1904 the Corinthians inflicted a record defeat upon Manchester United which stands to this day, demolishing them 11–3.

Nobody can doubt the talent which could be found within their ranks, as testified to by an Austrian opponent, after the Corinthians had played against his side in an exhibition game in Vienna: 'I remember how they walked on to the field, spotless in their white shirts and dark shorts. Their hands in their pockets, sleeves hanging down. Yet there was about them an air of casual grandeur, a haughtiness that was yet not haughty, which seemed intangible. And how they played!'

There were still occasional encounters with professionalism, not least among them an annual match against the winners of the FA Cup, which in 1904 brought them up against Bury, who had swept Derby County aside in the final, 6–0. It was a mark of how strong the Corinthians were that they in turn demolished Bury 10–3, but it was also one of the last games of its kind.

It was only once they began to enter competitions that they stopped being little more than a practice side – a training opportunity for the England amateur squad. They were the finest collection of amateurs of their day, drawn together for a common purpose, with club success coming only as a late and almost coincidental side effect.

The start of the 1907–08 season triggered a series of events which were to have profound consequences for Woosnam, when they joined the Southern Amateur League. Troubled by what they perceived to be the growing strength of professionalism, the Corinthians had broken away from the Football Association to form the Amateur Football Association. This split the amateur ranks, reducing the number of teams, their quality, and consequently the number of high-class, competitive matches. The amateur nose had been cut off to spite the professional face.

First they attempted to persuade the FA to form their professional base in Manchester, leaving the amateur set-up untouched and unchanged in London. Thankfully for the future health of the game the FA refused, minimising the effects of the split the Corinthians seemed determined to cause. While the FA banned its clubs from having anything to do with the unaffiliated AFA, it also retained leadership of its own clubs, preventing them being run by the well-meaning but dangerously impractical men who were leading the Corinthians and their counterparts into footballing exile.

Woosnam was particularly frustrated by the lack of

football this afforded him, and annoyed at the inflexible stance the Corinthians had taken. He played just five matches in his debut season for the Corinthians (1912–13) and a pathetic two the following year. He had played more football back at prep school than he was managing now, and were it not for the matches he played at Cambridge, he would have found himself in virtually premature retirement. The situation was leading him to draw determined conclusions about the value of amateurism.

As the isolation from serious competition dragged ever onwards, Woosnam became convinced that it was increasingly pointless for amateurs to lock themselves away in ivory towers, loftily decrying any contact with professionals, while watching their sporting activities wither away as a result. He was a pragmatist and a sportsman, and refused to accept a set of sporting ideals which led a man to engage in less sport than he had before. He was also unwilling to accept that the matter of one's amateur status should trouble anyone beyond the individual concerned.

Fired by this belief, he used his ever-increasing varsity reputation to help influence the Oxford Union to align itself with Cambridge and retain their membership of the FA. A joint universities team played against a selection of league clubs, and the success of the matches kept the relationship between the paid and unpaid versions of the game on a far better footing than would otherwise have been the case. Amateurism may be, by nature, a conservative movement, but driven by Woosnam's pragmatism, a degree of common sense re-entered the discussion.

The Corinthians' belief that even the merest brush with professionalism would result in desperate damage being done to football meant they were prepared to move away into an amateur enclave of their own, notwithstanding the damage this was doing to the state of the game. Had Woosnam not campaigned to minimise the exodus of clubs to its ranks, the game would probably have been damaged even more.

One repercussion of the AFA's independence was the European Football Association's refusal to allow any side not affiliated to their English limb to play in their country. The Corinthians, in their desire to protect their overly restrictive version of amateurism, had scarcely a European opponent against whom to play, and it was their solution to this problem which led them to Brazil.

Football was a very different game in the early part of the twentieth century from the one we know now. The light-weight boots players use today would have been of little use attempting to propel the leather ball Woosnam used, mud-caked, roughly stitched and growing heavier with each drop of water its leather coating absorbed. Similarly, the pitches of today, mown like billiard tables, would have been wasted on the boots Woosnam wore – ankle-high, hard-soled, little more than leather workmen's boots with leather studs nailed into the sole to help provide traction through the muddy wastes. Gusto was more important than guile, strength favoured over subtlety, the nature of the ball meaning every-day parts of the game such as headers and volleys involved a degree of reckless bravery.

Equally, and befitting the nature of the ball and the state of the pitches, the physical side of the game ensured tackles were made routinely that in the modern game would result in not just dismissal but prosecution. It was a game for strong, hard men, played in a brutal style in uncompromising conditions. Max Woosnam was a privately educated, tennis-loving university student. That anyone paid him the slightest attention on the pitch, let alone took him seriously, is a testament to his talent.

He had enjoyed a fruitful if brief first season for the Corinthians, with five goals in his five games from centre-half suggesting he could be a fearful presence in the area at set pieces. Given the physical nature of the game, his goals also tell us something more about his competitiveness and his physique in comparison with other, more mature men of the time.

A engaging account of the Brazilian tour of 1913 is contained in F.N.S. Creek's *A History of the Corinthian Football Club*, published in 1933. While players may be treated like passing royalty today, could any of them honestly claim to have experienced anything quite as colourful as a Corinthian tour abroad? From Creek's description, it appears unlikely:

Leaving Southampton on 1 August 1913, the Corinthians travelled via Vigo, Lisbon, Madeira, Pernambuco and Bahia to Rio, which was reached on 18 August. It was rather an adventurous voyage.

Cutter only caught the boat at the expense of leaving his luggage behind, while to relieve any monotony on board the proceedings were enlivened by a wedding, a birth, two deaths (one a suicide) and the escapades of a cook who suddenly went mad.

Of the three matches played at Rio, the first was lost, rather unluckily, by two goals to one, Woosnam scoring the visitors' goal with a fine shot from twenty yards' range. For the second game, the three 'veterans' Morgan-Owen, Day and Hoffmeister were introduced, and the effect of this was quite astonishing.

Their experience of tropical conditions resulted in a marked improvement in the Corinthians' play. Morgan-Owen completely subdued the centre-forward who had been so dangerous in the previous game, while Hoffmeister scored all the four goals of the afternoon, three of them as a result of excellent play by Day.

It is difficult to imagine quite how the 'tropical conditions' must have felt to a man born in Liverpool, brought up in North Wales, and having been forced to endure the freezing bathing conditions of Horris Hill. Suddenly, the pitches were hard as rock, lacking much grass, and the ball bounced head-high and above. The heavy-duty boots, so essential for traversing muddy English pitches, felt like divers' boots on the hard, South American ground, while the heavy kit, so handy for keeping away the worst of the cold at home, left the players feeling like they were trying to play football while wearing blankets. Having proved his worth at the physical side of the game, Woosnam's first senior tour saw him faced with a far quicker, more skilful version.

For a boy from the quietest parts of rural Wales to have become such a success at Winchester and Cambridge was one thing, but travelling to Brazil must have been a dizzying culture clash. The noises, the smells and the sights were like nothing any of them had ever seen before; eighteen days on a cruise liner had brought them, quite literally, to a different world. Rather than attempting to offer too much of an insight into the effect these strange, new conditions had on the players, Creek settles for writing about matters on the pitch. The results he reports suggest that they adapted better than one might have expected:

> For the remainder of the tour, with the possible exception of the last match, which was drawn, the Corinthians were definitely superior to their opponents, although they found it harder to win their games than in 1910 [when they toured previously]. In the third match at Rio, goals by Day and Woosnam resulted in a two goals to one

victory, a score which does not adequately represent the tourists' advantage.

The excellence of the hospitality extended defies any attempt at description; and the fact that the attendances varied from six thousand to ten thousand proved that the Corinthians were still very popular visitors.

They were certainly popular, and while touring through necessity rather than choice, given their lack of opponents elsewhere, the Corinthians were making an impression. They had visited Brazil, three years before their 1913 tour, and inspired the formation of Corinthians Paulista. The idea was to launch a side not limited to the descendants of British workers and settlers, but open to anyone wishing to play the game. Following in the steps of Flamengo, the Corinthians were among the very first popular Brazilian football teams. By 1914 they were state champions, and they remain to this day the second largest side in Brazil, behind only Flamengo. If English football had turned its backs on the Corinthians, the Brazilian game opened both its arms and its hearts to them.

♔ ♔ ♔

Upon arriving back home, as if to emphasise his discontent with the Corinthians' policy of strict amateurism, Woosnam sought additional footballing opportunities, a quest that soon took him off in a surprising direction. He was an educated man, and while polite and charming, he was never blindly deferential. In the years to come, he was to make a number of decisions which showed, both to his credit and sometimes his detriment, that he was not scared to stand up for himself, and to demonstrate that he would not be dictated to. His desire to show the amateur authorities that payment was a personal, not a general issue, led him to a place where, many years later, the issue of money in football would once more be hotly debated.

Chelsea Football Club were just nine years old in 1914, having been formed specially to fill the otherwise empty Stamford Bridge stadium designed by Archibald Leitch, the eminent architect of the early twentieth century, who drew up the plans for, among others, Anfield, Goodison Park, Highbury, Roker Park and Villa Park.

The Chelsea player-manager through those early days, from 1907 right up to 1933 (by which time his playing days were long behind him), was David Calderhead. It was Calderhead who spotted Woosnam playing at university and, hearing of his problems with the Corinthians, offered him a mutually beneficial solution. In the event, Woosnam turned out for Chelsea on just three occasions at the tail end of the 1913–14 season, but having endured another rather barren year with the Corinthians, it was an opportunity which he felt unable to resist.

His debut was on 21 March 1914, and typically he

managed a victorious introduction, helping the side to a 1–0 win over Derby County at the Baseball Ground. On 28 March 1914, Woosnam took his place in the heart of the Chelsea defence at Stamford Bridge, and repelled his future side Manchester City, as Chelsea recorded a 1–0 win. A fortnight later, on 11 April, he helped his side keep another clean sheet, as Chelsea beat Blackburn 2–0, again at Stamford Bridge.

They were to be the only three games he played for his 'new' team, as university demands carried him back to Cambridge, without allowing any further time to develop his role at centre-half. He had played through 270 minutes without seeing his side concede a goal, but his studies had curtailed the experience. Chelsea Football Club were a pleasant distraction, but if he was to earn a living he had to gain an education, and playing football at Stamford Bridge every week was hardly going to help him do that. Truly, it was a different age, as Penny Kavanagh recalls:

> He had nothing against professionals, and he campaigned very hard for amateurs to play alongside them, but he believed that everyone, regardless of whether they were being paid to play the game or not, had certain standards to uphold, and a code of behaviour to follow. He believed that very strongly, and much of what you see today would cause him to rub his eyes in disbelief. And not a little sorrow and anger as well, I should add.

When you look at some of the young men who play football today, with all their money to burn, they throw their weight around something rotten and their manners are appalling. When I saw those two yobs fighting on the pitch last week [this was in the wake of Lee Bowyer and Kieron Dyer's fracas while playing for Newcastle], well, my father would have had a fit, an absolute fit. If he saw what was happening today, he wouldn't believe what he was seeing. He refused to accept that being a professional meant behaving any less properly than if you were an amateur.

While playing for Chelsea, Woosnam did manage another game for the Corinthians – appearing against the English Wanderers on 25 March. The *Chelsea FC Chronicle* of the time shows Woosnam lining up at centre-half for the Corinthians in a game played, by coincidence, at Stamford Bridge, due to kick off at half past four on a Wednesday afternoon, with the sides numbered from one to twenty-two as was the practice of the day (Corinthians claiming the lower numbers and Wanderers the higher). One of the linesmen on that occasion, a Mr C. Wreford-Brown, had awarded an Oxford Blue to Woosnam's uncle Hylton some twenty-five years earlier. In those days, officials, in all their many and varied forms, were drawn from much the same pool – a select and prestigious group.

The various articles contained within the *Chelsea*

Chronicle apply a pleasing gloss to the ongoing arguments between the amateur and professional games:

> The appearance of two Cambridge university players in the match against Derby, R.H. Callender for Derby and Max Woosnam for Chelsea, is one of the happy effects of the reconciliation between the Football Association and the Amateur Football Association. And in either case the amateur proved himself to be fully up to the standard of first class league football, in no way suffering by comparison with the best of his professional confreres.
>
> The Cambridge captain, Woosnam, who filled the gap in our half-back line, was as good as any half on the field, and his fellow Blue also created an excellent impression on the home team's left wing. That next season will once more see amateurs being capped for the big international games is more than a little likely. Certainly varsity players will not be short of experience through lack of 'invitation' from league clubs generally.

He faced Manchester City next, retaining his place at left-half, with the game this time kicking off at four o'clock on a Saturday afternoon and attracting twenty-five thousand spectators, while a fortnight later, with the kick off dragged back half an hour to half past three, no fewer than fifty thousand turned out to watch Blackburn Rovers visit. As if to emphasise that there is rarely anything totally new happening in football, the debate about the permanently changing kick-off times and their effect on crowd numbers was alive and well even then.

In a later edition of the *Chelsea Chronicle*, Woosnam's performance in the Blackburn game once more received glowing praise. As the author of the piece stresses, had Woosnam been willing to remain at Stamford Bridge, Chelsea would have been more than happy to accommodate and welcome him. For a committed amateur, however, there was nothing to be earned out of football, and with an eye to the future he headed back to Cambridge, and his 'studies'. He also provides a further reminder of the nature of the game in which Woosnam participated. Modern-day football may be faster and more skilful than ever before, but in terms of sheer physical menace, players from the turn of the last century were encouraged to be as robust as possible:

> Few people expected us to beat the undisputed champions of the season, Blackburn Rovers, and none, surely, that our lads would beat them as handsomely as they did. Seeing that the Rovers had only suffered six defeats out of thirty-five league games it was without doubt the best thing the Chelsea team have accomplished the whole season through.
>
> Our amateur half-back, Max Woosnam, thoroughly enjoyed himself. What a worker he is! He will be all the better when he learns to use his broad shoulders a bit in a true Corinthian 'charge'. He refrained rather too

scrupulously on Saturday, and, as a consequence, the Simpson-Shea combination were inclined to do a little unnecessary 'show' work occasionally. Nothing like a 'touch' of the shoulder to stop antics of that description! Anyhow, if the Cambridge captain does not earn a cap before he is much older many good judges will be surprised.

At the age of twenty-two, then, he was good enough to play for the Corinthians, the country's finest side, as well as for Cambridge, yet still with room to become even more combative, a real footballing 'hard man'. It is hard to think of too many current footballers who would have relished getting in Woosnam's way as he launched himself, wearing his workman's boots with their nailed-in leather studs, into a challenge.

There are also a few words reserved in order to complain about an incident where the ball may or may not have crossed the line. Ninety years before they were to be ousted from the Champions League by a Liverpool goal they claimed never crossed their goal line, Chelsea were feeling aggrieved about one of their own efforts being ruled out for failing to creep over Blackburn's:

What is more, there is no doubt that the real score was 3–0, and not 2–0. Everyone thought a third goal was scored, and a loud shout arose when the ball was scooped out (almost from the back of the net it appeared from the stand) and our amateur captain, the last player in the world to entertain 'notions' on such a subject, has no doubt the ball crossed the line by at least a foot. But what did it matter – under the circumstances! It was a glorious victory, and every player is entitled to a full share of the credit.

Doubtless at the time the question of whether or not a football passed through the plane of a chalked line appeared desperately important to all concerned, but such arguments were merely distractions from the troubles of a wider increasingly unstable world. On 28 June 1914, three months after Woosnam played for Chelsea and less than a month before he returned to Brazil for another Corinthian tour, a chain of events was set off that altered lives forever.

CHAPTER FOUR

A BRUTAL INTERLUDE

After another blissful year at Cambridge collecting varsity victories and earning further Blues, the twenty-two-year-old Woosnam was looking forward to a return trip to Brazil with the Corinthians, who were planning a follow up to their tour of the previous season. If their previous trip had been taken out of necessity, their return journey was a much more popular prospect with the players and hosts alike. The news that Gavrilo Princip had stepped out of a Sarajevo coffee shop and assassinated the Archduke of Austria, Franz Ferdinand, while mildly troubling, had little impact on the genteel pace of university life, and it was difficult to see how it might influence anything Woosnam and his colleagues were about to do. No one predicted quite how swiftly events would spiral out of control and the world be brought to the brink of war.

In the circumstances, hopping on a boat to Brazil in order to play a bit of football with one's friends, was a plan never likely to run along the smoothest of rails. As

F.N.S. Creek recalls, with an understatement which borders on the comic:

> It is misleading to apply the word 'tour' to the last of the pre-war missionary journeys made by the Corinthians; rather should it be called an exciting sea voyage.
>
> On 24 July 1914, a party of fourteen left Waterloo for what was intended to be the club's third visit to Brazil; but within a week, rumours of war eclipsed all thoughts of football. On 6 August, a message was received announcing the declaration of war, and the course was immediately altered, as a German gunboat was supposed to be waiting on the regular route.
>
> At Pernambuco, Cockburn, Wilkinson, Tetley and Fosdick left the party. They were members of the Reserve of Officers, and had to take the first boat home. Two days later, *HMS Glasgow* stopped the ship in order to purchase some stores, and on the next day Rio was reached. The party had only time to walk up and look at the football ground before it was necessary to re-embark on the *Aragon* for England.

Had Charles Woosnam survived, he would have been in position, with his regiment, and become the first of the family to head off to war. With Charles dead and with his father's position as chaplain to the forces, Woosnam knew what was expected of him, as, it appears, did all of the Corinthians:

The return journey was slow and adventurous, as the German cruiser *Bremen* was reported to be in the vicinity. There was tremendous excitement when Lisbon was reached on 26 August; every bit of war news was eagerly devoured. Three days later the *Aragon* arrived off the Lizard; a torpedo boat fired a shot across her bows and told her to proceed to Tilbury instead of Falmouth. Time after time during the voyage up the Channel, the *Aragon* was held up in the dark by transports crossing; but at last she reached port and the Corinthians got back to London.

By force of circumstances, all the Corinthians put aside all thoughts of football to undertake the more serious task of fighting for their country. Their fortunes are not known, but of that happy party who set out in July 1914, only one was ever to tour abroad with the Corinthians again, and three at least only hurried home eventually to make the supreme sacrifice. The pre-war era, with all its implications, was over.

That the Corinthians enlisted, to a man, is not surprising, especially in the heady first months of the war. Their whole sporting ethos owed almost everything to high principles and the concept of the rounded human being – of there being more to life than sport alone. It also marked them out once more as being different from the Football League sides with whom they had been in dispute for so long. The league season of 1914–15 was played out to its conclusion before clubs released their players to go and enlist for the war effort.

As a result of the footballing authorities' unwillingness to curtail the season prematurely, the senior masters of the nation's public schools came to the conclusion that the game should be viewed as unpatriotic. There may not have been conscription at that point, but examples had to be set, and football's was a poor one. As a result, football lost a huge amount of support in public schools, where tradition is all and change happens slowly – a situation which has only recently started to correct itself.

Within a day of returning to England with the rest of the Corinthians, Woosnam rushed straight back towards Aberhafesp and joined up with the Montgomeryshire Yeomanry on 30 August 1914. The Yeomanry was part of the South Wales Mounted Brigade, a regiment which, since the Boer War, has served overseas and with which the Woosnam family, through the Canon and the household staff, had historic connections. Woosnam joined as a Second Lieutenant, the family groom and coachman joined up with him, and they stayed together throughout the war, serving alongside each other in Turkey, Egypt and France.

Woosnam was amongst the 300,000 men who enlisted in the first month of the war, buoyed by the calls of Lord Kitchener, the new Secretary of State for War. In September the number had leapt to over 450,000. Spirits were high, there was work to be done and a war to be fought. Things changed swiftly, however, as soldiers were slaughtered in huge numbers and enthusiasm inevitably evaporated. By October 1914, the number of new recruits had plummeted back down to a little over 100,000, and Kitchener would be forced to look at other, more aggressive campaigns to persuade men to enlist. But for the time being, bravery, bravado and ignorance were the recruiting sergeant's greatest allies.

Initially, Woosnam and his battalion were posted to Aldeburgh, in Suffolk, in order to prepare for a posting to an as yet unidentified overseas location. His days of enthusiastic training in the late summer were further brightened by a relationship with a young woman called Edith Johnson, the youngest daughter of a Scottish book publisher, to whom he became engaged.

He was plainly well regarded by those in command and, not for the first time, his ability to get along with people and mould together a team became apparent, as he was promoted to Temporary Lieutenant on 16 May 1915, just before his first major experience of war. Using leadership skills learned on the playing field, Woosnam soon found himself on a notorious battlefield. On 10 October 1915, accompanying the 1st Mounted Brigade, he reached what is now known as Anzac Cove on the Gallipoli peninsula in western Turkey, and joined the 54th Division in the wake of a mass slaughter that had been going on for the last five months.

The Gallipoli debacle stands as a distillation of the catastrophic early months of the First World War. The original plan, formed by Winston Churchill as First Lord of the Admiralty, was for the Allies to seize control of the whole Gallipoli peninsula, thus gaining control of the Dardanelles and striking a massive blow against Turkey and their allies the Germans. It was a clever idea, but lack of planning, incompetence and under-estimation of the Turkish army saw the subsequent campaign take a bloody place in the military history books.

The initial landings, on 25 April 1915, went about as badly wrong as they could have done. At Cape Helles, at the south of the peninsula, the British troops were met by heavy Turkish fire and struggled to disembark as their comrades fell around them. The Australian and New Zealand troops at Anzac Cove on the western side managed to reach the shore unharmed, before discovering that they had landed at the wrong place; ahead of them lay mountains, ravines and the Turkish army.

Confused and beleaguered, the Allies followed the same tactics as they had on the Western Front: they dug themselves in, and the Turks did likewise. And there they stayed, fighting and dying, as spring turned into a scorching summer, and then into a wet and dismal autumn.

The assault on Gallipoli was led by General Ian Hamilton, an experienced Scottish soldier who, as the weeks dragged on and the death toll rose ever higher, grew keenly aware that the plan had turned into a disaster. 'The beautiful battalions of 25 April are wasted skeletons,' wrote Hamilton, as the corpses piled higher and disease began to sweep the area, bringing yet more death. Kitchener came to see the site for himself, hoping to find some light at the end of the tunnel, and some way to present the situation as a delayed triumph, but a triumph nonetheless. It was a hopeless task and even later reinforcements, including Woosnam and his comrades, made little difference.

Retreat was the only solution. Woosnam's regiment was withdrawn in November, and early in the morning on 9 January 1916, the last contingent of Allies departed, leaving their dead behind. The evacuation was portrayed to the public as a tactical masterstroke, and an example of British military planning, but no one, least of all the soldiers involved, was convinced. From the carefree days of school and university sporting triumphs, Woosnam had been plunged, along with hundreds of thousands of others, into hell.

After Gallipoli his regiment was transferred to Egypt, where they arrived in December, before joining the Western Frontier Force in February 1916. It was to be a final act for the Yeomanry, who survived another year before amalgamating with the Welsh Horse Yeomanry to form the 25th Royal Welch Fusiliers, complete with its traditional spelling.

Woosnam was again promoted, this time from Temporary Lieutenant to full Lieutenant on 1 June 1916. His promotion was no doubt the result of another man's death or injury, an all-too-common fate in this time of total war. Prior to his promotion, Woosnam was allowed some further home leave, and took the opportunity to return to England and make wedding plans. Edith was a woman, as Penny Kavanagh proudly remembers, with an indomitable spirit.

> A lot of, I don't know what you'd call it – our 'never say die' attitude, I suppose, came from my mother's side. It was the French influence, if you like. An awful lot. The French have a much different attitude to many things, and they refuse to be beaten, which is something I see as lacking from the English attitudes towards things these days.
>
> She was a terribly practical woman, and she got the ball rolling when we had a farm running, with chickens and sheep and the like. She was a proud and strong woman, although she never felt the need to try and shout and scream about the work she had to do, because that was neither her way nor the way of the time. We could learn a lot from looking back at how we behaved then, I think.

Max and Edith were married in February 1917 – quite probably, from the descriptions offered of both of them, because they seemed like the only two people on the planet with sufficient drive, determination and energy to deal with each other. The honeymoon was brief, and soon Max was back at war, being promoted to Acting Captain in April.

By the start of June 1917, General Allenby had become Commander-in-Chief of the Egyptian Expeditionary Force, and set about preparing his men for a new offensive. The War

Cabinet in London had decided, and were intent on making it crystal clear to the men on the ground, that the 'highest importance' was attached to the need to 'strike the Turks as hard as possible'. Given their experiences at Gallipoli, one would have forgiven Woosnam and his fellow soldiers for feeling deeply suspicious of new and enthusiastic plans to 'strike the Turks', but the plan appears to have been followed with all the keenness the War Cabinet had hoped for. Before being dispatched, the troops were allowed a brief period of home leave, at the start of August, in order to rest and recuperate after the exertions of the previous months.

On the troops' arrival back in Egypt, the regimental records reported that intensive training continued through-out a summer of 'uncomfortably high temperatures and the prevalence of disease'. The descriptions of events in Egypt serve only to remind that horror, in the context of the First World War, was a relative concept:

> Fortunately, despite the conditions, the health of 25 RWF remained good. Training was interspersed with raids on the enemy positions, one by the battalion resulting in the killing of seven Turks. Allenby, by the skilful use of deception, planned to lead the enemy to expect the main attack against Gaza while delivering it to Beersheba, twenty-five miles to the south-east.
>
> 74 Div. was involved at Beersheba when the battle began on 31 October. 25 RWF advanced over a rolling

plain and were met by a hail of MG bullets every time they breasted a rise. By 10.40 a.m. they were within six hundred yards of the Turkish lines when forced to lie in the open whilst the artillery tried to destroy the wire. The heat was tremendous and casualties mounted.

At 12.30 p.m. the order to assault was given. Cpl J. Collins was conspicuous in rallying and leading his command. He led the final assault with the utmost skill, in spite of heavy fire at close range and uncut wire. He bayoneted fifteen of the enemy, and with a Lewis gun section pressed on beyond the objective and covered the reorganisation . . . he showed throughout a magnificent example of initiative and fearlessness. For his gallantry he was awarded the Victoria Cross, the first such award in the Theatre. Beersheba was taken and the battalion went into reserve. It had captured 140 prisoners whilst suffering over two hundred casualties.

By the time Gaza was finally secured, on 7 November, the Turks had suffered heavy losses. The next stop for Woosnam's regiment was Jerusalem, with the Brigade ordered to take over Beit 'Ur el Foqa, ten miles to the north-west. Having advanced silently under cover of pre-dawn darkness on 30 November, the brigade, under the command of Major J.G. Rees, and with eighty British troops, found the town heavily defended, with the Turkish soldiers inside in the middle of cooking breakfast:

Within minutes 450 had surrendered, 300 of whom were escorted back to British lines. The sixty remaining men were strongly attacked and practically surrounded. At 8 a.m. and down to thirty men and four officers [one of them Woosnam], Rees gave the order to break out and join up with the British line, which they achieved by 9.45 a.m.

For the battalion, it was a victory which led to a final conflict in the region, some four months later, when, having spent three months building roads and surviving the intense heat, they were thrown into the battle of Tell 'Asur, which opened on 8 March 1918:

> The 74 Div. attack was made astride the Nablus road on the ninth. The advance was soon held up and activity not resumed until after dark. 25 RWF deployed in the bed of the Wadi Nimr. The objective, Lisaneh Ridge, was not reached until 3 a.m. on the tenth after an extremely arduous advance, but carried after a sharp hand-to-hand fight. During the afternoon they succeeded in defeating two strong counter-attacks.

Quite how Woosnam and his men prepared for the heat of Egypt, where the sand mixed with the smell of death and fear, we will never know. All he knew of hot weather came from a couple of weeks' playing football in Brazil and, just as they had been at Gallipoli, things were now considerably hotter and unimaginably more frightening. By the time they arrived at the Lisaneh Ridge, after arduous, hand-to-hand fighting, the mental scars caused by the things they had seen and done must have been almost as bad as the physical scars they had collected along the way.

The victory provided only the very briefest moments of respite. Less than a fortnight later, on 21 March 1918, the great German offensive began in France. At the start of April the decision was made to replace all British troops in Palestine with Indian ones, in order that the British might be moved back to France to help counter the German assault.

As an officer, Woosnam was involved in the smooth running of the move, and remained in Palestine for several months after it was first ordered, to ensure the transition of Indian troops went without a hitch. It meant he was a long way from home on 8 May 1918 when Edith gave birth to Denise, their first child. It was a sign of the uncertain times that Woosnam found himself married and with a child before he even started his first job. If he appeared to be growing up more quickly than might be the case today, it was because world events were leaving him little choice. There was little point in putting things off until tomorrow, when tomorrow held no guarantees that you would reach its end.

The delay in moving the troops from Egypt meant that Woosnam did not arrive in France until October 1918, although while in the Middle East he did serve alongside a Royal Welch Fusilier officer of some renown, Siegfried Sassoon. Sassoon was already well known, as a result of his views on the war as expressed through his poetry and in a letter he wrote to a commanding officer which had been published in the press and read out in Parliament. He had been a keen cricketer in his youth, and though several years older than Woosnam, they would doubtless have had mutual acquaintances through the social circles which surrounded public school and varsity cricket. Although Sassoon had also enlisted at the earliest possible opportunity, even before war was officially declared, the brutal elegance of his verse expressed his growing horror at what he saw.

It is hard to imagine that Woosnam had much sympathy with Sassoon, never having had much time for what he would undoubtedly and brusquely have concluded was something akin to half-heartedness. Once he was set to a course of action, deviation, even when caused only by intelligent reconsideration, was not an option. His burning belief that 'life should go on' drove him forwards. In Woosnam's world, personal responsibility was enough to keep things in neat order. Regardless of the importance of Sassoon's message, or the quality of his poetry, it is hard to resist the idea that Max Woosnam would have felt some disquiet about someone making public their concerns, especially in the way that his fellow officer had done.

When Woosnam arrived in France the main thrust of fighting was over, but he was not too late to avoid the discomfort of the trenches or sporadic passages of hostility. Even in the very last days of the war assaults were launched which carried with them the very real risk of death or serious injury, such as the one described by Max's Major, W.N. Stable, on 18 October 1918:

> At 0830 the Battalion with a Battery of 44th Bde RFA and one section of MGs continued the advance, acting a Advanced Guard to the Bde. 'B' Coy commanded by Lieut. Woosnam provided the Vanguard at Ad. Gd. and was held up in the village of Sainghin by enemy cyclists and Light MGs.
>
> This enemy screen was driven through the wood and across the Marcq river where the enemy established himself in a strong position on the high ground east of, and commanding the crossings of, the river – the bridges over the river being blown up. 'D' Coy under Lieut. Robinson cooperated on the left flank of 'B' Coy but all efforts to get patrols east of the Marcq river failed.

The danger of the situation, sanitised by the use of bland phrases such as 'held up', rather than the more accurate 'fired on repeatedly by machine guns', becomes clearer in the reports of the following morning's events, when the Major is seemingly less keen to stick to such neutral military phraseology: 'Touch had been lost with the enemy, but was re-established when a patrol was sent out to seek a position further down the east road only to be driven back by MG fire.'

By this stage of the war, there was a deep sense of weariness about proceedings. All the horrors one could ever have feared had been seen, and death had become a perpetual visitor to the trenches. Even the most dramatic and tragic entry in the daily log is described in a clipped and specific manner that seems almost designed to preclude any lengthier consideration of the subject, as if a product of the officers' need to retain control and calm in the midst of chaos and carnage. The constant presence of death must have threatened the sanity of the troops just as much as their lives, and heroism was no guarantor of safety, as shown by the entry for 24 October: 'Lieut (Act. Major) Beavam awarded DSO for gallantry displayed in Somme operations on 18 and 21 Sept. Pte. M. Condon DCM (since killed) was awarded military medal for gallantry during same operations.'

With that piece of ceremony over, matters returned to the fighting which, in the last two weeks of the war, was no less fierce. Woosnam's battalion suffered a dozen casualties, but for the men on the ground, 5 November brought a hint that the end might be near:

> During the night information was received that according to the statement of a Prisoner of War captured during the day – the enemy intended to withdraw during the night. Therefore on completion of relief, patrolling was vigorously carried out but the enemy was found to be holding his posts in normal strength.

The troops must have prayed that the information was accurate. Two more days passed without further developments. And then, just as it must have seemed that the enemy PoW's story about a withdrawal was little more than a cruel hoax, on 8 November 'A patrol sent out at about 0300 found that the enemy had withdrawn. Other patrols were immediately pushed out and it was soon found that the enemy had withdrawn all along the front.'

The days which followed consisted of forward sweeps through territory which had been defended vigorously for weeks and months beforehand, only to have suddenly been deserted by German troops. Finally, on 11 November, the news which must have been so desperately awaited made its way through to the front:

> At 0830 the 231st Bde continued the advance – The Advanced Guard was under the Command of Major W.N. Stable M.C. and consisted of 25th RWF with one troop of the 19th Hussars – two sections of MGs and a battery of the 44th Bde. RFA.
>
> The Brigade was marching to the vicinity of Ostiches from where the 25th RWF were to move forward and establish a position on the high ground in vicinity of canal I.5 – I.10 – I.15.
>
> The march was very well carried out and when marching through the liberated villages en route much joy amongst the inhabitants was evident.
>
> About 1400 Battalion had reached Perquiese where a halt was made while reconnaisance [sic] was carried out with a

view to selecting an outpost line for the night. At 1500 information was received that an Armistice had been signed with Germany and hostilities had ceased at 1100 that morning. Thereupon Battalion was withdrawn into billets.

For hundreds of thousands of men, this announcement meant the difference between life and the prospect of imminent death. More than four terrible years of fear, of horror, of the ever-lengthening lists of the fallen, were over at a stroke. In their place remained horrific memories, bitterness and guilt that for many survivors – perhaps Woosnam included – lasted a lifetime.

For the next few weeks, the troops went through the process of preparing to return home, and, unit by unit, departing back to England, trying to pick up the pieces of civilian lives they could surely hardly remember. The trauma and mental suffering they had endured was not fully appreciated in 1918, when a stiff upper lip was often seen as more important than a sympathetic ear.

There were myriad reasons for any soldier to be grateful for escaping alive and whole from the hell of the trenches. Most of the men departing for England were looking forward to leading 'normal' lives once more. Woosnam had spent more than four years away from his lifeblood, sport. For him, a return home meant a return to Cambridge and to a raft of extraordinary feats just waiting to be achieved.

CHAPTER FIVE

AN ENGLISH HOPE

For today's teenagers, brought up in the age of satellite television, football stretches into the summer, cricket starts in the spring and ends in mid-autumn, and rugby league is a game of dusty pitches and hot weather. For the generations before them, different sports occupied set places in the calendar, and as if carved in stone, remained there. At school a love of sport grew up around a strict, formalised framework – two terms of winter sport, one of summer and a long holiday where you continued to avoid football or rugby until school restarted and the ground began to soften slightly.

In essence, September to April saw winter pursuits, and May to August summer pursuits. It was a schedule which had been passed down through the years, and which, unwittingly or not, provided the earliest opportunity for Max Woosnam to demonstrate the breadth of his talents.

While his footballing abilities were never seriously doubted, it was during the summer months that he enjoyed his greatest triumphs. With the ball at his feet, or shoulder to shoulder with an opposing centre-forward, Woosnam was a talented and popular centre-half, glorying in the physical side of the game and earning the respect of just about everyone with whom he played. The same cavalier spirit which so endeared him to football fans made him an even bigger name in the world of tennis.

Tennis had always been a part of Woosnam's sporting landscape, rather than something he migrated to involuntarily when his winter pursuits came to their annual conclusion. Oddly, perhaps, he does not seem to have played the game to any particular level while at Winchester. The likelihood is that, too distracted by cricket, he never picked up a racket competitively until reaching university, restricting his tennis to holiday fun back in Aberhafesp.

There was certainly a greater momentum surrounding his drive to master the game as a result of beginning to play seriously at a later stage, and he made the leap from varsity-level tennis to the most senior ranks of the sport with characteristic surefootedness. Upon leaving Cambridge in 1919, Woosnam would have been forgiven for feeling a few nerves, as he waited to see if his game was good enough to be competitive at the highest level.

As it transpired, his debut performance at Wimbledon was rather mediocre. A first-round victory in the Gentlemen's Singles against Mr Youll, an English player who left such a meagre mark that even the Championship's computer cannot now recall his initials, saw him through to a match with Wilfred Heath of Australia who disposed of Woosnam in straight sets.

But his lack of success did little to quell the interest that was beginning to surround his name in the press. Woosnam, 'the famous amateur', was never destined for anonymity and a man who had just survived the horrors of the Great War was never likely to be thrown by a few excitable words in a newspaper. As the *Daily Mail* proved, the modern-day practice of hyping young English tennis talent in the press is nothing new:

> Woosnam is the Admirable Crichton of sport. First class at lawn tennis, cricket, football, golf, real tennis, and racquets. Multiple Cambridge Blue. Best amateur centre-half since Mr Wreford-Brown, but prefers lawn tennis to all other games. The epitome of physical energy. An English hope.

Because of his very recent emergence from the genteel world of university sport, even in defeat Woosnam still attracted attention. In *The Times*, much like the *Daily Mail*, the praise was meted out regardless of the score:

> Max Woosnam, Cambridge University's all-round athlete, and a rising sun on the horizon of British lawn tennis, made a heroic fight against R.W. Heath, of Australia, in the centre court yesterday. But he has not

quite enough experience to prevail against such an opponent.

The greatest crowd of the week watched on, and they were heart and soul with the blue-eyed, golden-haired Englishman, who performed prodigies of court covering, but lacked the knowledge of tennis tactics to press home victory.

While they were rose-tinted in their coverage, the newspaper reports held enormous significance at the time. There was no television, scarcely any radio, and newspaper reports were much more influential on public opinion than is now the case. The press 'liked' Woosnam, and his tennis was generally well praised, but public acclaim was harder to achieve – at a time when Englishmen actually won tennis matches, hardly anyone had the opportunity to watch them.

Partnered with Newton Thompson in the Gentlemen's Doubles, Woosnam again came up against Heath, this time in the first round and with Heath playing alongside the prodigiously talented Randolph Lycett. Having battled gamely before losing the first set, Woosnam and Thompson claimed the second to level the match, before going out fighting, losing the next two sets. The pairing went on to reach the final of the plate competition, but were beaten. It is hard to imagine that what was effectively a 'consolation prize' for first-round losers meant very much to Woosnam, however sportingly and politely he concealed his feelings.

He gave a slightly more impressive performance in the mixed doubles, as he partnered Edith Greville through to the third round, before being beaten by Albert Prebble and Dorothea Chambers. Chambers had first won an All-England title in 1903, claiming the singles crown as Miss Dorothea Douglass. Although coming to the end of her competitive career, she was still a player to be reckoned with, described the previous year by the *Daily Mail* as 'the ideal ladies' player, driving with beautiful rhythm and strength'.

Although it was his first major tournament, Woosnam would have expected to have done better than to leave all three competitions before the end of the first week, but the experience would go on to benefit him in the coming years. While the press still heaped praise on him, for his amateurism and all-round ability, he was taking a calmer approach, well aware of the leap in class playing at Wimbledon represented and planning how he might continue to improve. He needed more experience at the highest level, that much was clear, and if he was to make the most of his potential, he needed to set about accruing it as swiftly as possible.

In the run-up to Wimbledon, Edith had given birth to their second daughter, Penny, and life in the Woosnam home was every bit as hectic as Max's sporting life had become out of it. In the aftermath of tournaments, he sought refuge from the heady pace of life he had been leading, or so he told Edith, when he announced that he was taking the family to the seaside for a break. Conveniently enough, the holiday

coincided with the Eastbourne late-summer tennis tournament, and Woosnam entered the gentlemen's singles and
doubles as well as the mixed doubles. As the redoubtable
Lawn Tennis and Badminton magazine recorded:

> Very little difference was to be found between pre-war and
> post-war conditions at Eastbourne. The Devonshire Park
> courts looked as perfect, and played as perfectly as ever; the
> entry was of the mammoth proportions to which those
> who know their Eastbourne have become accustomed.
>
> The megaphone was even more lustily employed than
> ever, and with as little effect, for players, many of them
> quite new to tournament conditions, were more difficult
> to find and get into court than in the old days. But
> everyone – or nearly everyone – at Eastbourne takes the
> rough with the smooth, and the handicap players bide
> their time with exemplary patience, knowing that their
> reward will come in the second week, when the levels are
> over and done with.

Lawn Tennis and Badminton magazine provides something
of a soundtrack to Woosnam's tennis career, such is the
frequency with which he appeared within its pages. Its words
invoke an age of dinner-jacketed broadcasts, clipped accents
and large gin and tonics. Published on a fortnightly basis, its
pages contain a jumble of part-finished prose and a plethora
of statistics crammed into every available space in eye-
wearying eight-point print. Where other publications might

comment on a misprint in the programme of events, *Lawn Tennis and Badminton*'s decision to dedicate three paragraphs to what it describes as a 'typographical inexactitude' sums up its sporadic pomposity.

Possibly because of the influence of a doubtless hassled and harried Edith, Woosnam withdrew from the singles before the tournament got under way, but, partnered by Noel Turnbull in the men's doubles and Mrs H. Cobb in the mixed, he finally found the form which had eluded him at Wimbledon. Although he gave a creditable performance in the mixed doubles, reaching the quarter-finals, it would quickly be overshadowed by his achievements with Turnbull. Having been given a bye through the first round, they sped through the next two with a minimum of difficulty, losing a mere handful of games along the way.

In the fourth round they knocked out Colonel A.N. Dudley and N. Mishu, described as 'a dangerous pair', an opinion supported by the fact they had failed to lose a single game in their run thus far. Woosnam and Turnbull were into their stride, however, and went on to progress through to the final without conceding a set, much to the approval of the press: 'The victory of Woosnam and Turnbull (they won against Stowe and Owen and are accordingly in the final of the doubles) should go a long way to raising English hopes for future international contests.'

In the final they continued their run of form, defeating G.T.C. Watt and C.O. Tuckey in straight sets. Watt and

Tuckey had yet to drop a set in the tournament, and had come through the semi-final without even conceding a game, but never came close to upsetting Woosnam and Turnbull. 'Woosnam and Turnbull did not lose a set to any pair, and in the final they had a very easy victory over Watt and Tuckey, who had, up to that stage, played very well, but never got going against the winners.'

In the 1920s, tennis looked and was played differently from the game we know today. Men wore long trousers, women long skirts, and things proceeded with a certain dignity. Serving and charging into the net was unheard of, as a step backwards to commence a baseline battle was the standard tactic, regardless of the surface. Coming off court, the men would don three-quarter-length smoking jackets, straighten their cravats and make sure they looked properly respectable.

If the crowds fell in love with Woosnam for daring to be different, it was not for his dress sense, as he remained as determinedly smart and dapper as the next man, but for the extraordinary way he flung himself around the court. Harking back to his mother's insistence on playing backhand, for fear of losing a point for decorum's sake, Woosnam flew around the tennis court with great energy. He dived for shots that others allowed to pass, chased down lobs that should have been winners, and hurtled after serves into the net, in order to launch volleys. If he wasn't as polished and neat as other players, he made up for it with his general athleticism. Whatever the game, Max Woosnam ignored the conventions which dictated how he should play, and adapted his talents as best he could. It was highly rewarding.

Eastbourne rounded off a successful end to an unusual summer of tennis for Woosnam, who was growing, week by week, into a bigger fish in a much bigger pond.

But still, life as an amateur meant the need to find work was now a priority. For professionals today, there is no question of getting a job after Wimbledon comes to a close. Were the top names never to win another point at the championships, the rewards they gain through sponsorship alone are sufficient to afford them a living more comfortable than most could ever begin to aspire to.

For Woosnam, amateurism meant travelling out into a world beyond the baseline. It would be wrong to think of him as some kind of a martyr, tramping out into the workplace to fight amateurism's battles – had he wanted to earn a living out of his sporting abilities, he was one of the few who could have done so. At the same time, his need to do more than just play sport all day long is precisely what makes him an interesting character, and is the central point of Woosnam's story. His determination to remain steadfastly amateur, and the impact this had on his family life, remains as strange to our eyes as ever it was. Needing to work, and unwilling to turn his hobby into his profession, Woosnam headed north.

He applied for, and was offered, a job at Crossley Brothers, a famous Manchester-based engineering firm.

Crossleys already owned several premises in the Manchester area, and shortly before Woosnam joined them had purchased further factory space in Nottingham. It was an expanding, successful business, and in addition to the Nottingham venture, they had also just regained a factory of their own which had spent the last few years being used by the government in order to support the war effort. The factory still produces engines to this day, but the name of Crossley, after a series of takeovers and changes, no longer appears on their side.

Such was the interest his prowess had generated, that as soon as word of Woosnam's move up to Manchester became known, he received two offers to further his footballing career. John Robson, then holding the eccentric role of secretary-manager at Manchester United, was keen to sign him up, having followed his exploits for the Corinthians and heard of his performances for Chelsea in the year before the war, while the Manchester City manager of the time, Ernest Mangnall, was also keen to enlist the new arrival.

Mangnall had, until 1912, been in control at Manchester United, and had guided them to some of their earliest successes. He was known as a colourful character – a manager ahead of his time, who enjoyed dealing with the media and whipping up interest in his side and their achievements.

He earned United promotion from the Second Division in 1906, and when City were hit by a financial scandal shortly afterwards, necessitating the sale of several of their squad, he was first in the queue to claim a host of influential players. Among them was Billy Meredith, who had been banned from playing for eighteen months in 1906 following the City scandal, as rumours of bribery and corruption swept the town. Mangnall saw the situation develop, from Meredith starting his ban, through City fighting their punishment, and let the days tick away towards its end before swooping for the player as City's appeals failed and Meredith was once again free to play.

Meredith went on to star for United for fifteen years, becoming a hero to the crowds with his dazzling wing play and eye for goals. For his part, Mangnall brought about the beginning of a golden era at United, guiding them to a Charity Shield, a League title and an FA Cup triumph, while seeing them installed in their new home at Old Trafford, but it was not to last. His flamboyant style was always destined to rub certain directors up the wrong way, and when he left in 1912, there was only one destination sufficiently dramatic and controversial to welcome him, as he marched out of the red and into the blue.

Woosnam was fully aware of Meredith's experiences with both clubs, and sought his advice on which offer he should take. Meredith, believing United's demise to be inevitable, directed Woosnam towards City. Much to the delight of Mangnall, it was advice Woosnam heeded, and on 7 November 1919 he signed for the club. As the *Manchester Evening News* reported:

An unexpected and welcome accession to the ranks of Manchester City is announced today: the well-known amateur, Max Woosnam, who was captain of the Cambridge Association XI and captained the south against the north last season. He is of fine physique and should greatly strengthen City's half-back line.

Mangnall himself kept his own counsel about the signing, content to enjoy the satisfaction of having pulled off something of a coup from under the noses of his former club and City's bitter local rivals. In subsequent years, though, he did expand upon the behind-the-scenes movements which helped him to land his man:

He was then registered as an amateur player for Chelsea, and he assisted them whenever he could make play fit in with the multifarious demands on his time. When the Chelsea directors heard that Max had accepted a business appointment in Manchester, my friends Claude Kirby, the chairman of the Chelsea Club, and David Calderwood, the secretary, wrote me immediately suggesting that Max would probably like to get a game for us as he was so passionately fond of football, and if so they would be very pleased to send along his league transfer.

I hastened to have an interview with Max, and he told me he would willingly play for us. He pointed out, however, that he would only be able to play in the home matches for business reasons. At that time he could not undertake any away matches.

There was a curious development in the matter. When it came before my Board in October they declined the offer. I knew what an acquisition to the team Max would be, and from that loyalty I felt duty bound to secure the player so that other clubs in the locality who were our rivals might not have his assistance in matches against us. I therefore persevered and took it upon myself to register him and the Board confirmed my action when I reported it at the November meeting.

I do not think anyone will blame me for taking the initiative in capturing the famous Blue who would have been lost to the Manchester City club.

Then as today, rules occasionally have to be bent, or at least temporarily ignored in the rush to sign an important player, and Chelsea will always go out of their way to assist anyone intent on upsetting Manchester United.

Despite his relative youth, and his lack of first-class footballing experience, there was a huge local clamour to watch Woosnam make his debut for City, which once again stands testimony to the power the newspapers had over the public. There was no television and the first live radio commentary of a football match was still almost a decade away, so the print media alone sent out the message, amplified through word of mouth, that Woosnam was a player to get very excited about. As Mangnall recalled:

> I have known time after time when the arrival of Max
> Woosnam in a town has been regarded as a social function
> in itself. People have just swarmed round the team on
> arrival and have excitedly asked if he were with them.
> It was the rule of Max, owing to the pressure of his
> business calls, to leave Manchester by the very latest train
> possible whenever he undertook to play away with us.
> Consequently the team were very often ensconced in
> some hotel before Max had set out by a late or an
> overnight train.
>
> It was when he was likely to arrive, say in some south
> Wales town, very late at night or in the dark and early
> hours of the morning that I have known the hosts of hotels
> to willingly wait up in order to welcome him. There was
> a breeziness about his big fine form and personality that
> brought with it the freshness of the fields; the atmosphere
> of the realm of pure and invigorating British sport.

Frustratingly for the Manchester public, however, he retained
some personal doubts about his fitness, and his readiness to
play at first-team level. Thanks to the policies of the
Corinthians, he had precious little competitive footballing
experience under his belt that season, and while he was
reaching full match fitness he wanted to play in the reserves,
so that people would not judge him until he was playing at
his best.

His first outing in City colours was in a reserve game at their home ground of the time, Hyde Road, and the *Manchester Guardian* was keen to ascribe the lion's share of the credit for the subsequent victory to their new signing:

> There was a remarkable game at Hyde Road between City and Blackburn reserves. City had their new amateur, Max Woosnam from Cambridge University, who acted as captain and played as centre-half. He had a great deal to do with City's victory.

Hyde Road was at this stage very much enmeshed into the psyche of City supporters. It was more than just a home ground – it was a home; somewhere that offered physical evidence of what it was that the club meant to its fans. Unfortunately, in among the warm words spoken about the ground was a cold, harsh reality – Hyde Road was growing more ramshackle by the week, and bits of it were hardly fit for crowds of any real size to gather in. There was also the question of a lease, which, by the time Woosnam signed for City, had only four more years to run, and was already costing the club more than five hundred pounds a year. Understandably, the directors could see little point in throwing money at a ground which might only be theirs for the very immediate future.

The *Manchester Football News* was particularly outspoken about the condition of Hyde Road – doubtless because of the frequency with which they had to experience its facilities:

'The croft is a nightmare in wet weather, and altogether the approach is the easily the worst of any I know.' The *Hull Sports Mail*, however, even with the benefit of almost ninety years of hindsight, were getting a touch hysterical about the whole affair, describing Hyde Road as: '. . . a small, cramped, clammy affair. Some teams, when playing there, declared they could not breathe.'

Regardless of the surroundings, though, and despite a slightly stumbling start to the season, which saw City concede twenty-seven goals in their first ten matches, things were beginning to look up. Woosnam spent his first few months looking on from the reserves at a side building its own confidence just as he was building his own fitness. Having been heralded by the local papers, keen to witness him in action for the first team, he finally made his debut on 1 January 1920, at home to Bradford City, helping the side to a 1–0 victory. Inevitably perhaps, given the result and the fervour with which they had campaigned for his inclusion in the side, the local paper concluded he was 'a pronounced improvement at half-back'.

He made his next appearance in a 4–1 victory over Clapton Orient in the FA Cup, and popular opinion was united in its hope that Woosnam would help fill a half-back position which had long been considered a weakness in the side. City had developed a reputation as a dashing, dynamic team, with exciting wingers and forwards, but they also committed defensive errors that had often cost them dearly.

With results continuing to improve since Woosnam first claimed his place in the side, excitement was beginning to grow among the local fans as the next round approached, away to Leicester at the end of January 1920. But Woosnam withdrew from the side at a late stage, as work commitments mounted, and he chose not to request the time off, but instead scratch from the game.

Missing the solidity and stability Woosnam offered them, City were the surprise victims of a 3–0 defeat by Leicester, and the fans' shock swiftly turned to anger. Rumours began to sweep around the area that Crossley Brothers had refused him the time off, and as such, found themselves blamed for the loss. Among those holding this mistaken belief were a number of employees of the firm, who promptly sent a message to the management outlining their upset and annoyance, and threatening to strike if such a situation arose again.

Feeling distinctly upset and more than a little confused at the turn of events, the board of directors summoned Woosnam. They explained, in a tone which didn't invite debate, that they would be grateful if there could be no repeat of the affair. He should consider himself obliged to play the next time City requested him, work commitments or not, lest the fans again start to believe that he had been barred from appearing. In essence, if Woosnam wanted to avoid the sack, he would be well advised to concentrate less on his commitment to his employers, and more on his service to his football team.

The future Olympic gold medallist, Wimbledon champion, England football and British Davis Cup captain, then aged twelve (front row, centre), with the Horris Hill school football team. Their expressions betray the harshness of daily life for boys in an English boarding school in 1904.

ETON v. WINCHESTER. JUNE 1910.

Woosnam (fourth from left, front row of standing boys), amply demonstrated his prodigious cricketing talents while at Winchester College, captaining the school team and scoring 144 not out at Lords, only to abandon the sport shortly afterwards as other challenges claimed his attention.

Sitting among his colleagues at Trinity College, Cambridge in 1913 (second from left, rear seated row), where Woosnam demonstrated that the footballing skills which had first raised their head back at Horris Hill, continued to develop as he prepared to enter the senior game.

With the first sighting of what was to become a very familiar moustache, Woosnam, while never convinced by the extent to which they supported their cause, was a proud and vital member of the staunchly amateur football team Corinthians, immediately prior to the First World War.

Woosnam's distant stare in this picture (above) taken while at Cambridge, was captured just months before he left the sheltered existence of university life to join the carnage of the First World War battlefields. He spent the next four years serving in, at various times, Gallipoli, Egypt and the trenches of the French front. Given the horrors he faced, the cartoon (below) drawn round about the same time, now leaves the word 'battle' feeling horribly inappropriate.

TO-DAY'S BATTLE OF THE BLUES.

The Captains Courageous—R. F. POPHAM (Oxford) and M. WOOSNAM (Cambridge).

While his Horris Hill team picture featured expressions which betrayed childhood sadness, the faces surrounding Woosnam, sitting second from the left in the front row, alongside the other men from his home village of Aberhafesp about to go off to war, now reveal genuine fear and apprehension.

Sitting with the ball, among his Manchester City colleagues in 1922. Captain of the side – an amateur leading professionals – he was described by a future City captain, Sam Cowan, as 'the greatest centre-half and captain Manchester City ever had.'

Even with the finest digitally enhanced colour photography, it is hard to imagine that modern newspapers will ever tell the story of a sporting event more charmingly than in this cartoon from Woosnam's days at Manchester City.

In the years running up to the Second World War, county tennis weekends offered Woosnam the chance to take Edith (top), Penny and Denise along with him. He did not always find the combination of sport and family so easy to manage, either while competing at the highest level, or in the years of sporting retirement which followed.

Even in retirement, Woosnam remained a familiar sight at tennis events, as did his trademark cigarette. His influence on the game remained strong, as he organised tournaments across the north of England, designed to improve the standard of doubles in the country.

Sporting retirement allowed Woosnam to concentrate on his business career. No longer fitting a full time job into his spare time, he flourished, ending up, with typical nonchalance, on the board of ICI; the sombre, pinstripe suit scarcely hiding his sense of vigour and excitement.

Woosnam addressing the crowd at Maine Road in 1958, before a fitness display provided the blue half of Manchester with what to modern eyes seems slightly surreal pre-match entertainment. He remained a hero at City, and had a street named after him, Max Woosnam Way.

As his name slipped from the public's attention, in the 1960s, this cartoon from the *Daily Express* sought to draw attention to his achievements, even if the likeness leaves something to be desired. Even in the form of a cartoon strip, they conveyed only half the story.

A report, carried by a local paper, in January 1920, after he had played against Middlesbrough – just his fourth game for the club – gave some clue as to why he was so prized. Under the flattering but less than catchy headline 'Max Woosnam's Brilliant Display at Manchester', the praise was lavishly heaped on:

> Nobody showed anything like the all-round excellence of Max Woosnam. The famous amateur was the outstanding player on the field. His effectiveness was compatible with his boundless energy. Strong alike in attack and defence, he was always in the thick of the fray, and so far as I know, there is no half-back so capable of taking the ball on the full volley and directing it with such accuracy. But in every respect Woosnam was masterly, and it is unquestionably his presence, coupled with the successful return of Brennan, that has brought about the very material improvement in the City team.

With such critical acclaim ringing in his ears, along with the advice of his employers that he play as much as possible, he turned out for all but three of City's last eighteen games of the season, which they finished in seventh place. Everyone had high hopes of a better start and an improved final placing in the season to come. Woosnam had brought some much-needed defensive qualities to the side, and as they continued to bond together, there was real optimism about the future. The fans knew of Woosnam's reputation, but the high quality and vigorous nature of his performances had still been a surprise. As far as Max Woosnam was concerned, the surprises had hardly begun.

CHAPTER SIX

MAX THE OLYMPIAN

Woosnam played his last football of the 1919–20 season on Monday 26 April, helping City to a 1–0 victory at Aston Villa in front of a crowd of over 45,000. While his colleagues went off to rest and recuperate, the summer of 1920 offered further challenges for Max on the tennis court, and one in particular which was to prove irresistible.

1920 saw Woosnam play less tennis than at any other point in his active career, and yet claim arguably his greatest triumph, at the Olympic Games in Antwerp. Wimbledon champions, England captains and Davis Cup skippers might come and go, but an Olympic champion occupies a special place in the sporting world and Woosnam's respect for this amateur festival of sport was heartfelt.

The reasons for his lack of tennis prior to the Olympics shine a light on the world of the 1920s amateur. He had competed on several occasions for the Lancashire county side, and was a gifted player, particularly in doubles, but the idea of spreading his wings further, and taking more time than was absolutely necessary to prepare for Antwerp was out of the question as far as he was concerned.

As the threatened strike by his fellow workers revealed, the relationship between Woosnam and his new employers had the potential to be very beneficial to him. As a result, he did not intend to cause any unnecessary friction with his superiors. In addition, after the arrival of his two daughters Denise and Penny, he knew that he had a living to earn and a family to keep – he had priorities in which sport did not always lead the way. As such, asking for time off for something as trivial as tennis was, to Woosnam's way of thinking, out of the question. He simply stored up the holiday he had owing to him, and looked to take it towards the end of the summer, in August, so that if selected, he might be free to travel to compete in the Olympics.

The 1920 games in Antwerp were only the sixth games of the modern era; as a result of the First World War, they had not been staged for eight years, since Stockholm. Woosnam's time at Trinity had made him acutely aware of their importance. Seven Trinity alumni had won gold in 1908, and two others alongside Woosnam were to do likewise in 1920. The Olympic tradition might have been a small one at the time, but it was still one to which Woosnam would have felt more committed than many others. He prepared as thoroughly as he could, while taking as little time off work as he could manage. The only other tournament he took this seriously was the nearby Lancashire Open, at which he won the singles title.

On 31 July 1920, the Lawn Tennis Association announced that Woosnam would be one of eight to represent his country, under the captaincy of R.J. McNair. Other team mates of note were his doubles partner Turnbull and Kitty McKane, who was later to become Kitty Godfree, and would go on to win two Wimbledon titles. It was impressive company for an amateur of limited experience to be keeping.

On the heels of this announcement came another which, while leaving Woosnam with a dilemma, provided a further insight into the man and his sporting mind. The Amateur Football Association announced their squad for the Olympics, and, aware that he was by some considerable margin the best amateur footballer currently playing the game, requested that he join the side with a view to captaining it. Juggling the two sports would be difficult, even by his own hectic standards, and the schedules all but made the decision for him.

In the end, it was with a degree of regret but with a healthy dose of realism and practicality that Woosnam thanked the footballing authorities for their invitation, but was forced to decline, either from captaining or participating. As with his decision to play tennis instead of cricket while at Cambridge, the great all-rounder had been beaten not by a lack of energy or talent, but by the clock. There simply weren't enough hours in the day for him to pursue all the avenues open to him.

It proved to be an intriguing football tournament – Czechoslovakia were trailing Belgium 2–0 in the final when they walked off in protest at a disputed decision, forfeiting the game in the process. France, meanwhile, shunned the bronze medal match, after most of their team despondently returned home after losing the semi-final. The Corinthian spirit, as misunderstood as it had become, was nowhere to be seen.

In July 1920, while he was still trying to prepare for Antwerp, mixing work and play as effectively as he could, one of the largest tennis stories of the year was played out in Eastbourne, as America beat France to claim the Davis Cup. The sides competed in the UK for practical reasons alone – the world's best players were already gathered in England to play at Wimbledon, and in the days before commercial airlines, travel was a lengthy, time-consuming process.

Differences in travelling times aside, though, the world of tennis seemed to be remarkably similar to the present day. A report in *Lawn Tennis and Badminton* of 17 July 1920 informs us that:

> As anticipated by many, there has been a large application for the debentures of the new ground where the championships will be played. As we go to press, we understand that the issue will have been over-subscribed, and no doubt several who have delayed sending in their applications will be disappointed.

The relationship between the sport of tennis and the

Olympic movement was weaker in the 1920s than it is now. The Olympics were not viewed by the tennis establishment as a tournament of any outstanding worth, albeit for entirely different reasons than exist at present. These days player power and the commercial demands of sponsors hold the whip hand in negotiations, but in 1920 national federations were all-important. With the tennis world revolving around Wimbledon, the LTA retained a grip on the control of the game despite the development of other nations, such as America and France.

The modern Olympics were less than twenty-five years old, and the British tennis authorities were perfectly happy for them to exist as a minor distraction. What they could not countenance was the games becoming sufficiently large to threaten the existing Grand Slam tournaments. While they were small, they would be viewed with a slightly patronising affection. If they grew larger, the position would require a little reconsideration. Meanwhile, there was little willingness from the British authorities to risk diluting their power and allowing the International Olympic Committee any real influence in the running of even a small, four-yearly part of the game.

Tennis had been part of the first modern Olympic Games in Athens in 1896, and was described in the official report as 'this most charming and athletic game'. Only men's singles and doubles were played at the first meeting, attracting an entry of thirteen players from four countries, and providing a platform for John Pius Boland of Ireland to become a double gold medallist. Boland not only won the singles, but having turned up without a partner, somehow persuaded the authorities to let him play alongside a German, Fritz Traun, in the men's doubles, thus earning a rare, if not unique dual-nationality gold medal.

Dublin-born Boland was an Oxford student of Greek mythology, who went to see the revival of the games purely as a spectator. He had a friend, however, Thrasyvoalos Manaos, who was Secretary of the Organising Committee, and who, knowing Boland played to a reasonable standard, entered him in the tennis competition. Despite having no plimsolls, and playing in leather-soled shoes with heels, Boland won, becoming an Olympic champion in the process. More than a century later, Nicolas Massu of Chile would collect the men's singles title at the 2004 games wearing Adidas tennis shoes for which we can safely assume he was paid a substantial sum. Winning an Olympic gold in training shoes may be more practical, but winning it in brogues will always be more romantic.

In the wake of such an ideal sporting victory, then, Woosnam set off for Antwerp. Officially the 1920 Olympic Games were awarded to Antwerp by the International Olympic Committee to honour the suffering the Belgian people had endured throughout the course of the First World War. In reality, they had won by default as the other contenders, Amsterdam and Lyon, withdrew, relieved someone else was footing the financial burden. Hosting the games was an honour, but in the days before sponsorship or television money, it came without hope of balancing the books.

If Woosnam had overcome minor inconveniences to make it to the games, arranging his holidays around the competition, they were trivial compared to some of the other participants. The Japanese team, all fifteen of them, made a journey halfway round the globe to reach their destination, before running short of funds before their return trip. Thankfully, a donation from two Japanese companies ensured they were able to make a safe, if slightly delayed return.

The Americans suffered even more acutely, steaming their way uncomfortably across the Atlantic on board the elderly freighter *Princess Matioka*, which had been used as a 'death ship' at the end of the war, transporting home American soldiers killed in battle. Upon arriving in port, the mood of the squad was not improved with the announcement that they would be staying on the boat, rather than transferring to a hotel. Amid the threat of something approaching mutiny, the American team's anger was eventually assuaged slightly, but they were far from a happy collection of athletes, despite finishing at the top of the medals table.

Some extraordinary black-and-white footage of the Games still exists, depicting neatly drilled ranks of athletes making their way around the track during the course of the opening ceremony, while a keep-fit display is performed with perfect synchronicity by thousands of participants on the infield. The athletes would in due course have to cope with a heavy, cinder surface, rendered almost unusable by some of the heavy rain which was to fall, but their marching, as was commented upon at the time, was impressive. Since almost every competitor had experienced some form of military service over the course of the previous years, this was perhaps unsurprising.

Given the constraints of time under which the organisers worked to get the Games ready, the numbers of athletes competing, although not vast by today's standards, was truly extraordinary. In total, the Antwerp Games attracted 2,626 entrants, for events as varied as rugby and tug-of-war, as well as a host of more traditional Olympic pursuits.

The men's singles tennis competition claimed forty-four of those entrants itself, and so it was that the first round saw Woosnam's introduction to Olympic competition, as he overcame a shaky start to beat Muller of Sweden, 3–6, 6–1, 7–5, 6–2. The conditions were desperate however, and the damp court did little to assist Woosnam's bustling game. His athletic style of play, diving and chasing around the court, worked well on dry days where his footing was guaranteed, but Antwerp's grass courts, once wet, were treacherous. There were also scheduling problems thanks to the difficulties of getting a grass court ready for play in wet conditions, and indeed the London Olympics in 2012 will be the first since 1920 to attempt to stage the tennis matches on the game's natural surface.

With conditions not to his liking, and having been selected more as a doubles than a singles competitor, it was not a surprise that he exited the singles competition just one round later, falling to the Spaniard Manuel Alonso, although his departure was less painfully protracted than some in the draw. Auguste Zerlendi, a Greek player, was drawn against Britain's Gordon Lowe, who would go on to become a Davis Cup colleague of Woosnam's.

The match between Zerlendi and Lowe lasted for five and three-quarter hours, an unprecedented duration in those days, and took up almost two days of court time. Commencing on Sunday evening, they played for two hours, by which time Lowe had claimed the first set 14–12. A further hour and a half on Monday morning saw Zerlendi claim the second 8–6, before the umpire announced, with an admirable sense of priorities, that he was calling a lunch break, as he was hungry.

They eventually returned to complete the match just before five o'clock, by which time both men had collapsed, at varying points, with cramp. Lowe unimaginatively called for a doctor, and after a massage was cured. Zerlendi, with a far more cavalier approach, called for beer and sugar, and consumed copious amounts of both. In a crushing blow for those who value romance over science, his 'cure' ensured he slumped, probably quite literally, to defeat.

Quite apart from the weather, conditions for the tennis tournament were far from perfect. The stadium was very close to the athletics track where the shouts and cheers of 30,000 people carried the short distance and echoed around the court. There was no hot water, nor were there any towels in the sparse changing facilities. But the evident enthusiasm of the competitors led to the event being declared a considerable success. Certainly, the Americans and the Germans, who had asked unsuccessfully for the dates of the competition to be changed to allow them to compete elsewhere first, were considered to have misjudged the mood.

With the singles competition no longer detaining him, Woosnam could concentrate on the doubles, which were and would remain throughout his career his speciality. Partnered with Noel Turnbull, who would play alongside him on many more occasions in the future, his performance failed to disappoint. Handed a bye in the first round, they raced through the second against the Italian duo of Di Robecco and Colombo, before overcoming the French pair of Decugis and Albarran in the semi-final.

Even given his reputation for modesty and understatement when asked to assess his own performance, Woosnam must have been nervous about the rewards victory would bring. If his life had already been lived at a frantic pace – from school to university to army, from Horris Hill to the varsity match – he was now, only months after starting his first job, on the brink of being an Olympic champion. After his first season in what would become the Premiership, he had spent the subsequent months fitting his summertime hobby around his work, and was now only one match away from a gold medal which, representing as it did the pinnacle of amateur achievement, plainly meant a huge amount to him. Only the Japanese duo of Kumagae and Kashia stood between Woosnam and his title. Having come this far, though, neither he nor Turnbull was ever likely to stumble, and as *Lawn Tennis and Badminton* reported, the gold medal was rarely in doubt:

> The men's doubles provided a fine win for Woosnam and Turnbull, who beat the Japanese pair, Kumagae and Kashia, by 6–2, 5–7, 7–5, 7–5. They might have won in three sets, but for carelessness in the second set. Woosnam's low volleys and service returns were the deciding factor.

This rather perfunctory description of an Olympic win says more about the way the competition was viewed than about the scale of the achievement. In an age where doubles partnerships were largely, though not exclusively, made up of a pair from the same country, the Olympics was as stern a test as any of the major championships.

Elsewhere in the competition, Suzanne Lenglen was confirming her position as one of the finest female players of her or any other generation, by storming to the gold, dropping just four games in four rounds. Woosnam, partnered by Kitty McKane, won his way through to the final of the mixed doubles, only to face Lenglen, who was partnered by Max

Decugis. On paper, Woosnam was just one victory away from claiming a second gold, but in reality, given the extraordinary athleticism and ability of Lenglen, silver was the most he and McKane could ever have expected to win.

Such was Lenglen's strength and power, even when masked by the grace and balance she brought to the game, that it was hard for another woman to come close to her. It was almost as if Woosnam and McKane played against an all-male pairing, for Lenglen would certainly have proved too much for several of the first-round losers in the men's draw. The French duo moved to victory 6–4, 6–2, and for once, it was genuinely reasonable for a British sporting team to feel that coming second was in itself a triumph.

It is also worth remembering that the competition was conducted at a pace which would seem utterly alien to today's competitors. Having won his gold medal alongside Turnbull in the morning, Woosnam played the final of the mixed doubles that same afternoon. Within hours, Woosnam had gone from not possessing a single Olympic medal to owning a gold and a silver. It was not a timetable for the fainthearted.

The foundation stones of Woosnam's extraordinary sporting story were now firmly in place. Coveted by Manchester City for his footballing talents, and having set his school and university ablaze with his all-round abilities, the events in Antwerp saw him take a huge leap forwards in terms of how he would now be perceived by the public.

At the age of twenty-seven, having demonstrated his extraordinary sporting talents at every opportunity, he had ensured that his achievements would be remembered forever. School victories and university accomplishments were one thing, but an Olympic title, even back in 1920, led him to new heights altogether. From the court in the garden at Aberhafesp to the Olympic final in Antwerp, his tennis journey, so often described in glowing terms, now encompassed an Olympic gold medal. For a confirmed and proud amateur, the prize must have been exhilarating beyond words.

For a man so ill at ease in the spotlight, modestly craving a degree of anonymity, things would never be the same again. He had arrived in the world of football as a famous sporting amateur, with people waiting to see if he lived up to the billing he had been given. He would return to it as an Olympic champion. If he was hoping things might settle down and some rhythm might return to his life when the new football season began, he was sadly mistaken.

CHAPTER SEVEN

CAPTAIN FANTASTIC

There was considerable pressure on Max Woosnam's shoulders upon his return from Antwerp. He had played just one season at football's highest level, and then only as a first-team regular for half of it, yet already the Manchester City fans regarded him as something of a hero. Now, with Olympic fame and titles to his name, it was clear he was to become a yet bigger star – and equally clear that this wasn't necessarily something he was prepared for.

While football had always been widely regarded as his strongest game, the events of Antwerp caused people, possibly even Woosnam himself, to reassess just where his greatest talents might lie. Playing for Manchester City was a huge honour, and one which he took very seriously, but he was in no way inclined to rewrite history and reinvent the reasons he played for them, just to bolster his own importance. Work, not football, had brought Woosnam to Manchester, and while he happened to be there, City had been a convenient and attractive option.

He had played just sixteen times for them, though, and when compared to the heights he had just reached with a racquet in his hand, he was still patrolling the foothills of the footballing world. He would never play sport for the money, but we should not confuse that Corinthian ideal with the assumption that he never played for the glory. His desire to succeed and to triumph was as strong as that of any professional, and the events of the summer had given him food for thought.

Realistically, a tennis injury was highly unlikely to keep him from playing football – the game lacked the physical risk that would have justified such fears. Football, on the other hand, could throw up any number of circumstances in which a player, particularly one who enjoyed the physical side of the game as much as Woosnam, could injure himself in a way that threatened a tennis career. He was known for his 'vigorous shoulder barge', and his willingness to get involved in the rough and tough of the game, and there was no possibility of altering his style of play to protect himself from injury. If the option was to play half-heartedly, then to Woosnam's way of thinking, it was no option at all.

If he was to live up to his promise, something had to be done, and so on his way back from Antwerp, letting his head rule his heart, Woosnam made a difficult decision. He would give up football, in order to investigate how fine a tennis player he might become. His tennis career had been littered with comments about how he might develop if he 'dedicated himself to the game', or learned its 'finer points'. Reluctantly, he decided to see if this course of action would benefit him. This decision was relayed to various interested parties – the press, the tennis and football authorities, and to his employers. Thankfully, both for English football, and all those with a sense of sporting romanticism, Woosnam left himself a major get-out clause – he would first re-sign for Manchester City 'just as a precaution'.

How those among the tennis playing fraternity reacted to this news is hard to say. As the local paper reported, with a distinct air of relief, Woosnam retained his allegiance to the club 'notwithstanding his declared intention to retire from football in order to devote his energies to tennis'. Many years later, Francis Albert Sinatra would retire annually on just such a basis, in order to better enjoy his comeback performance. With his half-hearted attempt at saying goodbye, Max Woosnam had to all intents and purposes achieved much the same thing.

It wasn't, it transpired, just the fear of a football injury which drove him to make the original decision, but also the amount of time he had to take off work in order to properly fulfil his obligations to both sports. Crossley Brothers were acutely aware of their employee's popularity, even without his Olympic achievements, and they now moved smartly to reassure him that they would allow his work to fit around his sporting activities. It was a decision which had benefits for the company beyond merely averting the threat of industrial unrest. Woosnam was fast becoming a Manchester legend, and his amateurism and modesty saw him singled out as a particular favourite among the factory-floor workers – the boy from Winchester and Cambridge had become a working-class hero. For Crossley it was a coup to have him working for them, and giving him the time off he needed to compete as widely as he wanted was a move motivated as such by business as by sentiment.

Affection for him was felt not just by his workmates and employers, but by the local media, as evidenced by the *Manchester Evening News*, whose reporter was moved to comment:

> When Max Woosnam told me at the end of last season that his future connection with the Hyde Road club, or any other football club, was more than doubtful because of his desire to play tennis, I experienced a pang of regret which must have been shared by all the supporters of the club, to say nothing of the many other people who found pleasure in watching his clever and exemplary play.

The passage is interesting not just because it offers a further glimpse into the way Woosnam was regarded, but also because of what it reveals about journalistic ethics of the time. Woosnam had told the reporter 'off the record' about his thoughts, and that trust had been respected throughout the summer, despite the value of the story. The article continues, 'These successes [in Antwerp] are calculated to wed him still further to his favourite game. He has, however, again signed an amateur form for City, and it has to be hoped that he can be prevailed upon to play the occasional game.'

Whether he believed he would ever need to be 'prevailed upon' or whether he had always intended to play for City as much as he could, once Crossley Brothers made it plain that they would assist him, Woosnam's decision to retire from football was obviously more than a little premature. He missed just eight games in the 1920–21 season, and five of those were at the very start, while he was still away competing in the Olympics. If being an amateur meant not receiving payment, it certainly didn't mean freedom of choice. Crossley Brothers employed Woosnam in no small part because they enjoyed the reflected glory he brought them, not to mention the publicity, and when he mentioned taking a break from his sporting exploits to spend more time at his work, he found himself being shunted neatly back out of the office door, and sent off in the direction of whichever arena required his presence. Woosnam was morally amateur, but effectively professional – he just received his orders from the owner of the local factory, rather than the owner of the local football team.

If Woosnam's change of heart regarding his retirement offered good news to the City directors, matters off the pitch swiftly darkened their mood. The start of November 1920 saw a fire at Hyde Road claim the only habitable stand, and reduce the much-loved but severely dilapidated old ground to new depths of shabbiness. Earlier in the year, United had offered them a ground share, but spurred on by a combination of pride and business sense – United wanted more in rent than City had taken in gate receipts the previous year – the offer was rejected.

Mangnall and his assistant, Wilfred Wild, in an 'all hands to the pumps' attitude, set about redesigning the ground as best they could, in order to keep the crowds and the money coming in. An embankment made of cinders was formed on the site of the old grandstand, which actually saw the capacity increased to 45,000. It was a haphazard development, though, and by the time the first game was played after the fire, against Huddersfield on 13 November 1920, the dressing rooms were still to be finished, and both sides changed in hastily installed washing facilities in the nearby Galloway's factory.

Having settled into the team and gone through this uncomfortable experience with them, one of Woosnam's earliest matches was the local derby against United, which ended in a 1–1 draw on 20 November after which the *Manchester Guardian* described him as 'the best of the lot'. The match was captured in cartoon form by 'P.S.M', the *Manchester Evening News* cartoonist, who produced a series of scenes from the afternoon which, almost a century on, still manage to convey the feel of the event. Among the images are an escaped dog which had to be 'arrested by an arm of the law', as a caricatured policeman stoops to seize a stray canine,

and the United goalkeeper John Mew, who 'had the opportunity of making some brilliant saves from Max Woosnam'.
In the bottom right-hand corner of the drawing is a picture
of a man in an overcoat and trilby hat, with the simple caption
'Ernest Tyldesley, the Lancashire cricketer was there'. It is
stunning to see an illustration which tells us about the events
of the day as effectively as these simple cartoons.

City went on to defeat United in the home leg of the
league fixtures the following week, with Woosnam claiming
yet more plaudits from the press. The *Empire News* reported
the game under the headline 'Woosnam the Master', going
on to record, 'Woosnam stood out by himself as the finest
soccer player on view, recording his finest game to date in
City's colours.' For a man who had considered retirement
from the game because of its risks, Max Woosnam was
playing some of the most ferociously physical football of his
life, and enjoying every barge and tackle.

With their season going smoothly if not spectacularly,
City needed a moment of inspiration from a key figure, if
they were to have a memorable campaign. Woosnam was a
crowd favourite and star performer, but as a result of his
workload at Crossley Brothers was unable to train with the
rest of the side. His relationship with his fellow defenders was
honed during matches, in front of crowds as big as 66,000,
but his leadership qualities and talents as a team player saw
him make precious few mistakes, and led his team to make an
extraordinary decision.

Unbeknown to him, the remaining members of the side approached Mangnall after training, while Woosnam was at work and unable to intervene, and requested that their amateur colleague be made team captain. It is an episode Mangnall recounted several years later, as he told the story of his managerial career to the *Empire News*:

Now and again one hears wild and irresponsible talk of professional footballers not liking the idea of amateurs playing on their side. Well, I can truthfully say during my career in the game I have never known a situation where the professionals have taken exception to any amateur player who was worthy of taking his place side by side with them.

If proof of this is needed it is contained in the story I am going to tell you which testifies to the respect the professionals playing with Max Woosnam had for him.

When he settled down as a regular player in our first team, Eli Fletcher, who was the captain, came along with other players to interview me. The request put forward by Eli on behalf of himself and his fellow players was that they would like to management to grant their desire that Max should be elected captain. I told them if that was their unanimous wish we had better approach Max and see what he thought of the proposition.

We did approach the famous amateur and he was so impressed by the sincerity and unselfishness of the players, their manifestation of esteem, and their compliment, that he accepted their tribute. The directors having fallen in with the suggestion, Max became captain.

There were never any regrets over the change in captaincy, for Eli and those who served under him or for the management of the club.

Woosnam was not a 'Fancy Dan' character, who charmed simple, less educated men. He was, as his record suggests, just as popular in every team situation in which he ever found himself. Nor was Fletcher a soft man, given to displays of emotion. He had lost three children in three years, including his only son at the age of just eighteen months, and throughout the ordeal he had played on and retained the captaincy. In the season he handed the captaincy to Woosnam he was forced to visit the dentist after a clash on the pitch, and had no fewer than sixteen teeth removed, before going on to play in the following match.

The captaincy decision was just the thing to boost City's season, and they went on to record eleven wins from their final sixteen games, with only one draw – testimony to the open and exciting style of football they played. Winning was what Woosnam understood best, and the concept of sitting back and settling for a point was anathema to him. City had given the current leaders, Burnley, a head start, but Woosnam was convinced that they could still catch them up.

On 26 March 1921, City played Burnley at Hyde Road, in one of the most extraordinary games the old ground was ever to witness. The home side triumphed 3–0, bringing Burnley's record unbeaten run to an end. The crowds were so desperate to get in to see the game that fences and gates were broken down, and while the official attendance figure remains at 40,000, estimates place it somewhere between 55,000 and 60,000.

City's cavalier style brought them to the brink of a tremendous recovery, only to slip up in the return match at Burnley a week later, having also lost to Middlesbrough in between. Burnley went on to take the title by five points, but City had run them closer than had once seemed possible. It had been a thrilling season, and Woosnam had proved his worth as an inspirational leader. At Hyde Road they went the entire campaign unbeaten, and amid the claustrophobic conditions it was Woosnam, white handkerchief tucked up his sleeve, who commanded the crowd's respect and admiration.

When questioned about his habit of carrying a white handkerchief up his sleeve – a footballing fashion statement that predated David Beckham's sarong by about eighty years and George Best's haircut by forty – he explained that while amateur shorts had pockets, professional shorts did not, hence through school and university he had acquired the habit of playing with a handkerchief in his pocket, to wipe his brow. The idea of playing in different shorts when playing for City, however, appalled him – he was the captain, and unity was everything – hence he played in professional shorts, with no pockets. The only alternative place for the all-important handkerchief, he explained in an interview with the *Manchester Evening News*, would have been inside the waist-band of his shorts, or stuffed down his shorts at the hip. As he said with a straight face, this 'would have made it look as though I had a growth in a most unfortunate spot'.

Although convention and a sense of propriety meant the majority of his public announcements were clipped, proper and polite, but there was another side to the man, the side that made him a cherished colleague in dressing rooms and on the training pitch. One-liners, rude jokes and innuendo have always been a large part of the mortar binding sports teams together. That little of this is recorded from Woosnam is down to his sense of discretion, rather than an inbuilt sense of seriousness. And when his sense of fun went a bit too far, Woosnam's ability to cause chaos was immense.

♈   ♈   ♈

The football season coming to an end, his thoughts turned once again to tennis. There was mounting speculation that, despite the questions being raised in the press, Britain might possess a collection of tennis players capable of competing against the might of the Americans, and challenging for the Davis Cup. In the early part of 1921, several newspapers reported that the initial, challenge rounds for the tournament, scheduled for early September, would all be held in the United States. This caused the Lawn Tennis Association to release the following statement on 26 February 1921:

> The statement which appeared in the press to the effect that the challengers for this year's Davis Cup had signified their approval of playing all the preliminary rounds in America is premature as far as the British Isles are concerned. The proposal is receiving the attention of the International Match Committee, but no definite pronouncement can be made on the subject until the draw has been published at the beginning of next month.

The days when Britain automatically ruled on all matters relating to the competition were beginning to fade, as more nations entered, and despite the strident tone of the announcement, there were private doubts about exactly how much influence the LTA still held in the wider tennis-playing world. By the time the next issue of *Lawn Tennis and Badminton* came out, it featured an announcement headed simply 'The Davis Cup':

> The draw for the Davis Cup is made as follows – First Round: Spain vs Great Britain; Canada vs Australasia; Japan vs Philippines; Czechoslovakia vs Belgium.
>
> The four nations which drew byes will meet in the second round as follows – Argentine vs Denmark; All India vs France.
>
> It is probable that at least five or six of the preliminary matches will be played in the United States.

The increased interest in the tournament is clear, but so also is the get-out clause 'five or six of the preliminary matches'. Which meant one or two might be played outside America, and everyone knew that Britain would be the first to take advantage of the flexibility. After all, they had been the ones to negotiate it into the draw in the first place, saving their own side from a trip to America, and allowing a climb-down from the organising committee which saved face all round.

Through means which are not now, and possibly weren't then, entirely clear, by the time the fixtures were reprinted a fortnight later, along with a report on the likely chances of the respective nations, the Spain versus Great Britain tie had become the Great Britain versus Spain tie. The Spanish side, in the wake of this rather unexpected change of location, might at least have consoled themselves with the prospect of playing at Wimbledon, or even a trip to the coast to allow Eastbourne to host the competition once more. A journey to an obscure part of North London was probably not at the top of their list, but like it or not, the fates and fixtures led them, in May 1921, to the oxymoronically named 'London Country Club', in Hendon, where the match claimed a small footnote in history as the first time in Britain that a Davis Cup tie was played on hard courts.

The team the Spanish sent to England was their strongest for many years. Manuel Alonso had beaten Woosnam in the Olympic singles competition, and only went out, a round later, after losing 7–5 in the fifth set to Noel Turnbull. In a six-game match against the French earlier in the year, they had drawn 3-3. But by the end of the first day of their encounter with England, the result was already as good as decided, as Randolph Lycett defeated Manuel Alonso in straight sets and Gordon Lowe wore down Conde de Gomar 6-3, 4-6, 6-1, 6-0. The home nation were left needing just one of the three remaining games (or rubbers) to take the tie, and Woosnam and Lycett teamed up in the doubles against Alonso and de Gomar to claim victory in four sets, and with it the match, sending the Great British side through to the final knock-out stage in the United States, where they were to face the Australians.

The rules of the tournament at that time decreed that the previous year's champion effectively 'sat out' the tournament, and waited to challenge the winner of the 'all comers' competition. Given the strength of the American side, whoever topped the group of challengers would have a hard fight on their hands, as *Lawn Tennis and Badminton* was quick to point out:

> Whoever earns that distinction, it will not be altogether an enviable one. America, with Messrs. Tilden, Johnston, Williams and Co. playing on their native turf and in their native climate, will present about the toughest problem that a challenger has ever had to solve.

Following their win over Spain, Woosnam and Lycett agreed to play together in that year's Wimbledon doubles, before setting off for Philadelphia to take on the challenge of the Australians. The championships were to be the last held at Worple Road, a ground which had now been outgrown for some time, prompting a search to locate larger, more spacious premises, with more opportunity to expand should the championships continue to grow in popularity. While the atmosphere there was impressive, with the close proximity of the spectators to the court, and the excitement generated by the crowd being pushed together into such a tight space, the downsides of the arrangement were beginning to outweigh the up. It also meant that the championships of 1921 were the last operating on the 'challenge round' system, which worked in the same way as the Davis Cup, with the previous year's winner missing almost the entirety of the next tournament.

As it turned out, the results of 1921 in themselves might have persuaded the various committees that it was time for an overhaul. In the ladies' singles, Elizabeth Ryan battled through to the final, before overcoming the memorably named Mrs Satterthwaite. One particularly acerbic reporter noted that the match was 'sufficiently described by the score, 6–1, 6–0 in Miss Ryan's favour. Against a volleyer of Miss Ryan's uncompromising type Mrs Satterthwaite had no chance. She was simply and swiftly rushed off her feet.'

Ryan's reward was to meet Lenglen in the Challenge Round, where she was promptly demolished 6–2, 6–0. The difference in class between Lenglen and the rest could hardly have been more vividly displayed, as Ryan was no mean competitor herself, winning her first ladies' doubles title in 1914, and her twelfth and final title in 1934. Nobody has ever won the event more often.

She also had something of a soft spot for Woosnam, according to an interview she gave during that year's Wimbledon:

> Max Woosnam is, in Miss Ryan's opinion, a delightful personality on the court. He is the one player who looks as if he is enjoying every minute of the game, and the sterner the tussle the more he revels in it. 'I know I look in fierce pain all the time myself,' said Miss Ryan, 'so I can appreciate Max Woosnam more than most people!'

Woosnam's campaign in the singles event ended once more in relative failure, disappearing from the competition in the third round, beaten in five sets by Cecil Campbell of Ireland. In the previous round Woosnam had defeated fellow Britain Drew Alexander, also in five sets, and the cumulative effort had begun to take its toll. While Wimbledon brought the best out of Woosnam, it also led him into a style of play which was prone to leaving even a man of his energies exhausted. Every ball was chased, nothing was given up for dead and, while it was a crowd-pleasing measure beyond compare, as the tournament went on, Woosnam inevitably suffered.

In the mixed doubles, he was playing with the little-known Phyllis Howkins, and with the draw finding them up against some of the best players of the era, the chances of them progressing beyond all but the first couple of rounds seemed remote.

The opening two rounds were smoothly navigated, but in the third round they met Dorothea Chambers and Bill Tilden in a match which, it was popularly believed, would end Woosnam and Howkins' run. Fortunately for them, with Tilden looking forward to what was to be a successful defence of his singles title, it seems that their opponents were less competitive than they might otherwise have been:

Woosnam and Miss Howkins survived their first severe test against Tilden and Mrs Mallory after a delightful match in which they both showed extreme cleverness. Tilden, it is true, was not taking himself very seriously; that, at least, was the inference to be drawn from his mien, which was light-hearted in the extreme – even for Tilden. It was the capture of one of his service games which enabled Woosnam and his partner to pull up from a losing position and ultimately win the final set amidst great enthusiasm.

In the course of the match, Woosnam made one of the most gorgeous flukes ever seen. He stuck his racket out at a hard smash of Tilden's and the ball came back – off the wedge – a perfect drop shot. Had it been met by the racket's face it would probably have fetched up somewhere in the region of the committee box! The match, in fact, teemed with amusing and exciting incidents, and the crowd loved it.

Had Tilden been more directly concerned about his progress through the mixed doubles competition, one suspects he might have turned the result around, but it was not to be, and Woosnam and Howkins moved through to the fourth round 3–6, 6–3, 9–7.

If people expected their next match would be a rather more serious affair against the formidable pairing of Percival Davson and Dorothea Lambert Chambers, given its standing as a Wimbledon quarter-final, they were to be pleasantly surprised: 'This was also one of those lively matches which the spectators enjoy as much as the players. Woosnam darted about with so much effect that a run of four games, and with them the deciding set at 7–5, was their just reward.'

Woosnam and Howkins' victory plainly caught the public attention. In an article published after the tournament, entitled 'Wimbledon Reflections' and authored by 'Hambledon', which rambles between the patriotic and the hyperbolic, it is clear that the progress of the duo was something of a highlight of the tournament, at least as far as the future of British tennis was concerned:

In the centre court on the last Wednesday I watched Woosnam of the smiling countenance, with his charming young partner, Miss Howkins, in their mixed doubles match against Davson and Mrs Lambert Chambers. It was young England versus the Old Brigade – and one's pulses beat the faster when one realised what this battle meant. Was it not typical of Britain, the mother of all ball games of today?

Under what other sun would such a contest have been possible? I see in my mind's eye the Woosnam and Miss Howkins of today on the centre court of the Wimbledon of 1941, handing on to Young England of that day the traditions which are their sacred heritage.

The last of the championships at their ancestral home is, to my mind, a triumph greater than the winning of every one of the championship events. The game for the game's sake has made lawn tennis what it is today. Britain in her missionary work the world over ever kept this idea in the foreground; and her reward was at Wimbledon this year, when men and women from every clime foregathered at the Mecca of their pilgrimage to add another chapter to the annals of the game.

After which, 'Hambledon' presumably went for a long lie down in a darkened room and commenced a lengthy course of intravenous pink gin.

The pair coasted through their next contest, against

Woosnam's Davis Cup opponent Manuel Alonso, and his partner Winifred McNair, in straight sets. One reporter observed that 'as speedy as he is, Alonso is not nearly so speedy as Woosnam, neither was he as sure over his shots'.

Despite the apparent strength of the opposition, it had been a relatively straightforward path to the final for Woosnam and Howkins, losing a solitary set over the course of five matches. Their victory over Alonso and NcNair, however, brought them into a final against the might of Lycett and Elizabeth Ryan, and a comprehensive 3–6, 1–6 drubbing:

> With Miss Ryan and Lycett on the very top of their form, playing accurately and brilliantly, Miss Howkins and Woosnam had no chance. They were simply smothered. Their ground strokes compared unfavourably with those of their vanquishers, who repeatedly scored outright with the return of the service. Three games in the first set and one on the second were all the losers could manage, and the score fairly represents the superiority of Miss Ryan and Lycett, who compare well with any famous pairs of the past.

While the general view appeared to be that the partnership of Woosnam and Hawkins had done particularly well even to reach the final of the mixed doubles, expectations for the mens' doubles were far higher. With Woosnam teamed with Lycett, few would have been willing to predict anything less than him finishing the tournament with a trophy to his name. *The Times'* pronouncement that 'in the men's doubles, although the entry was large, good pairs were somewhat conspicuous by their absence' did little to change that opinion.

Lycett and Woosnam should have faced a stern test in the very early stages of the competition, but the retirement of Gobert and Laurentz left them a relatively simple passage through to the last eight. In the other half of the draw a dearth of genuinely talented and experienced partnerships allowed the brothers Gordon and Arthur Lowe to make their way to the final, as they had done in 1914.

Almost without exception, the commentators of the day were convinced that the Lowe brothers were merely in the final due to the good fortune they experienced in the draw, and as such this left the competition somewhat devalued. The events on the other side of the draw, where Woosnam and Lycett were entertaining all who watched in a series of relatively competitive contests, received much more attention:

The semi-final, in which Barrett and Norton met Lycett and Woosnam, was regarded, perhaps rightly enough, as the virtual final, and it was hoped it would yield a fine match. But it did not. Lycett and Woosnam won with the loss of the second set in four.

Woosnam kept his end up well and so helped Lycett to do the rest. Barrett was not returning the serve as well as he sometimes can, but, apart from this, he was not making many mistakes. Norton, *per contra*, was making them by the dozen. He made some brilliant winners, too, but they did not lift his side up to the extent to which his errors let it down. When Barrett, the old campaigner, sometimes shook his head dubiously, volumes (as Dickens hath it) could not have said more.

Already the captain of Manchester City, an Olympic gold medallist, with a century at Lords to his name and playing golf off scratch, Woosnam was just one victory away from another major inscription in the sporting record books. Much as they might have wanted to, the Lowe brothers were never likely to stop him:

This was the first item on the last day's programme. Lycett began serving, and served accurately and fast, as he did all through, and crossed over 1–0. The next two games went with the service, but then Lycett and Woosnam won A.H. Lowe's service and led 3–1. Volleying keenly, they led 4–1. Service gave the Lowes the sixth game. A love game was the reply.

Lycett struck his only bad patch of the match in the eighth game, but made amends the next, which he and Woosnam won by vigorous attacks, and so the set at 6–3.

Lycett and Woosnam simply swamped the brothers the next set, winning it to love, Lycett's forehand return of the service being untakeable, and his smashing and volleying beautifully clean, severe and well placed. He dominated the play.

Whether Woosnam thought about the magnitude of what he was about to achieve, or indeed whether it even came as something of a surprise to him that he was going to triumph in yet another sport, we will never know. As a crowd favourite, however, and with his other sporting accomplishments well known, there is little doubt that, even in the refined surroundings of Warpole Road, he was going to move to victory through waves of cheering, even if his opponents were determined to make his journey to the title as difficult as they could:

> The third set was well contested, the Lowes hitting harder off the ground and lobbing well. Their policy was to bombard Woosnam. It succeeded so well that they led 5–4. But Lycett got busy, and going for everything, as did his partner, the Lowes failed to press home their lead and were beaten 7–5. It was Lycett's match; he played like a real champion and deserves the title. Everything he did was done superlatively well.
>
> Woosnam was safe, and, as usual, clever at picking up any kind of ball, but he needs more winning shots, a return of the second service, for example, that will either win

outright or produce a punishable reply. He served and smashed well, but was not always *en rapport* with his partner.

It was a rather anti-climactic way to report a victory which confirmed Woosnam's status as an all-round sportsman the like of which the world would rarely, if ever, see again. Two years out of university, and the sporting promise he had shown throughout his education was being realised, at the highest levels of his respective games. By the age of twenty-eight, and with four years spent at war, his achievements were already staggering. However, success meant little to him if it was not earned with the appropriate sort of behaviour, as Penny remembers:

> If he lost a match it was strange, because you expected him to win every game, every time, so it stopped being extraordinary. You never started to believe he would automatically win every time though, because that wouldn't have been right. Or perhaps I should say, even though you expected it, because that's human nature, you never expressed that thought, because that would have been dreadfully bad manners. It was a fine line between believing he would win and expecting him to.
>
> I suppose, thinking about it, they're the same thing, but believing tends to mean you keep it to yourself, which is

as it should be. Expecting it suggests that you were being quite vocal about what would happen, and we weren't, ever that. Partly because my father wouldn't have tolerated that sort of behaviour for one second, and partly because you were brought up not to behave like that in the first place.

I still look at people today on the television, telling anybody who will listen exactly what they're going to do and how great they're going to be and how far they'll win by, and I have to say I shudder a little. It seems so vulgar and so rude. It's just disrespectful and unsporting.

I can't see how you can demand respect for yourself, if you don't show it to others. It's not something about which you need to shout, but something that's best done quietly. When sportsmen really respect each other, they don't need to keep telling everyone, they just let their actions do the talking. That was certainly a lesson my father taught us.

In the immediate aftermath of the tournament, Woosnam was named as the captain of the Great Britain Davis Cup team, the youngest man ever to hold the position, and he prepared to travel with the side to the United States. They would have to safely navigate a difficult tie against the Australians if they were to have a chance of challenging a powerful American side for the trophy, and the press were not optimistic. Having been built up by the newspapers over the preceding couple of years, in the face of both Olympic and Wimbledon victories Woosnam and his Davis Cup colleagues were facing an uncharacteristically negative media:

> While everyone will heartily wish our Davis Cup team success in their transatlantic quest, no one can really expect them to be successful. They may be a good team, but not even their most prejudiced admirers would call them a great one, though each of the players has achieved the greatness which is conferred by being chosen for one's country. The same greatness carries with it the penalty of being criticised.

The author – and this was an article appearing in the official publication of the LTA, where one might expect a degree of support for the side – went on to pull very few punches when examining the quality of each individual:

> Max Woosnam, who captains the team, is a better doubles than singles player. To be quite candid, he owed his doubles successes at Wimbledon more to his partners than to himself. In the mixed, where he survived until the final, his partner, Miss Howkins, so disappointing in the singles, surpassed herself, whereas his own performances were decidedly in and out.

Then in the doubles championship Lycett was always master of anyone on the other side of the net. Nor was it a year of strong couples or a high standard of doubles play. So Woosnam should perhaps be accounted a trifle lucky to be a title holder. He is sure to be of that opinion himself, as modesty is one of his engaging virtues.

In the opinion of the correspondent of the magazine of the Lawn Tennis Association, Woosnam was lucky to be Wimbledon champion, playing poorly, aided by his partners and not all that great a singles player. His major strength was that he openly admitted it. After that less than promising start, the analysis began to brighten up, before reverting back to some more serious criticism of his form:

> In certain respects Woosnam has no equal in English tennis. He is a born athlete, with the physique, stamina and eye for success at all ball games, practically fatigue-proof, super-agile, a unique picker-up of half volleys, a grand trier, absolutely dauntless, and endowed with the merry heart that goes all the day. He is the very best type of athlete produced by the public schools and universities.
>
> Woosnam's first service is fast and very quickly hit; he gets it in fairly often. Overhead he is both sure and secure, and knows the value of smashing at sharp angles. Though

playing his volleys correctly and well, keeping the head of the racket well up, he does not attack with them as, for example, does Johnston, the American.

His return of service is safe, and well placed, played well down the middle, but a speeding up of his drives and volleys would greatly add to the effectiveness of Woosnam's game. He needs more devil in his ground strokes and volleys. If that were added to his other splendid qualities, he would be uncommonly hard to beat. The writer of these notes is not enamoured of his grip, which he blames for the special imperfection just referred to. Woosnam's play in the singles championship was hardly that of a Davis Cup captain.

It was a damning article indeed, but Woosnam accepted praise and criticism alike with a shrug and a smile, and never chose to object more vocally as many sportsmen today might. And, as history would go on to show, Woosnam's performances in the singles matches ahead were actually rather impressive.

♔   ♔   ♔

Preparations and predictions complete, the side eventually set off for the United States, having been joined by Woosnam in Liverpool, where they boarded the world's largest liner *Baltic II*, accompanied by the wives of Turnbull and Arthur Wallis

Myers, who was there in a journalistic role, as well as Woosnam's wife, Edith.

After their mauling in the press before departure, the ship's passenger log tells an interesting story of those travelling alongside the Davis Cup party. In the slightly spidery, black-inked handwriting of George Flemyng, a physician, trained in Dublin but working for the immigration department at Staten Island recording the passengers, some charming tales emerge.

Wallis Myers, a journalist and tennis writer of some repute, had produced several books on tennis tactics in the early part of the twentieth century. Whether he was responsible for any of the pre-journey articles about the side is impossible to say as they are, in the main, anonymously written, but he plainly enjoyed a reasonably courteous relationship with the players. Oddly, however, he did not travel on to Pittsburgh with the players, heading instead for an address at number 66 Broadway, in New York.

The passenger list gives clues as to who could afford to treat sport as a hobby, and who couldn't. Woosnam's doubles partner, Noel Turnbull, has his occupation noted as 'ship owner', and gives contact addresses in nice parts of Surrey and Hertfordshire. Lowe and Woosnam, from humbler back-grounds, both had their passage paid by the Lawn Tennis Association, while Turnbull's entry lists that his ticket was bought by 'self'.

The log records that the wives of Woosnam and Turnbull

both had their tickets paid for by 'husband', and that they would be in the country for six weeks. Much to the relief of all those wishing to avoid a scandal, all members of the party recorded their lack of support for polygamy, anarchy or violent revolution. Gilbert's ticket was also paid for by the LTA, but whereas the rest of the party stated they would be staying for six weeks, Gilbert only expected his trip to last for a month, suggesting that he already knew his role would be a limited one.

It seems slightly odd, in these days of showmanship and bravado, to read of a sportsman expressing doubts about his forthcoming prospects. But an interview given to A.W. Myers by Gordon Lowe hardly seeks to play up forthcoming British chances:

> Had it been possible to include Kingscote and Lycett [both of whom had declared themselves unavailable several months earlier], I firmly believe we should have reached the challenge round.
>
> All the same, it is a good thing, from many points of view, that young players are having their chance, as they can learn so much from their American experiences as to be of most valuable help for the future. From a sporting point of view it is much better that we should take our stand with other nations, rather than withdraw on the plea that we cannot have a fully representative team.

Max Woosnam is sure to be a very popular captain, and
I feel certain that under him we shall give a good account
of ourselves.

If this particular speech represents the peak of Lowe's abilities
as an inspirational orator, it is perhaps not quite so much of a
surprise that Woosnam was chosen to lead the team. Had
Lowe given the passionate team talk just before the start of
the tie, it would hardly have been worth the rest of the side
leaving the comfort of the locker room.

By the time the *Baltic* had arrived in New York, the
remaining first-round matches had been completed. It left
a second-round draw which paired Denmark against
Argentina, Japan against Belgium, India against France and
Woosnam and his team facing the might of the Australians,
with the United States waiting to challenge the eventual
winners. It had been a particularly stress-free tournament for
the Danes, Japanese and Indians, with their places in the draw
owing much to the simple process of entering the
competition, and then, one by one, watching their opponents
withdraw, thus claiming a walkover.

Australia and Great Britain had dominated the competition, along with the United States, since its first days. Of the
fifteen times the cup had been contested since the first
competition in Brookline, Massachusetts, in 1900, Australia
had won on six occasions, Great Britain five and the United
States, the current holders, four. Only once, when Belgium

lost 5–0 to Great Britain in 1904, had a country outside this trio even contested the final.

Whilst they must have read a great deal about their forthcoming opponents, neither the British or Australian side would have known all that much about the playing styles they were about to face. There were odd snippets of newsreel film, possibly showing a few strokes, or at best a rally, but in these pre-television days, unless a player had been seen 'in the flesh', the opinion of a reporter as to his abilities was as much as could be hoped for. Having said that, if the Australian team had picked up a copy of *Lawn Tennis and Badminton* and read up on the English side, they might have been too busy laughing and rubbing their hands together to concentrate on the game.

Eight years earlier, the magazine had run a feature on an extraordinary family of promising young Australian tennis players, the Andersons. There were six boys in all, each of them over six feet tall, with the youngest of them, J.O. Anderson, then aged seventeen, looking most likely to be a future star. Eight years on, now twenty-five, he carried the hopes of Australia, as he stepped onto the grass courts at the Allegheny Country Club in Pittsburgh, to face the reigning Olympic and Wimbledon champion, and opposing captain, Maxwell Woosnam.

Anderson had played in the competition two years earlier, winning a marathon singles match against A.H. Lowe, yet unable to stop his country from being defeated and the British retaining the trophy. Two years on and he was returning with both experience and a point to prove. It was a potent combination. The Australians had an inexperienced side, and there was a suspicion that they might not reach the levels they had done on previous occasions. This turned out to be unfounded.

On the morning of Thursday, 4 August 1921, Anderson proved that he had improved dramatically as a player over the course of the last two years. Both individually and collectively, it was to be a bad day for Woosnam and his team. Not, oddly enough, one which *Lawn Tennis and Badminton*'s correspondent seemed to think they deserved. Having previously doubted the wisdom of the team selection, the abilities of the players and the standard of their tennis, the moment they reached foreign shores, he seemed to feel honour bound to defend them wherever possible.

Although the Davis Cup archive records the result as a straight sets victory for Anderson, 6–4, 6–2, 6–4, the *Lawn Tennis and Badminton* correspondent takes the view that it was in fact a four-set defeat, and the 'spin' placed on the report of the match leaves the reader struggling to understand exactly how Woosnam managed to lose:

> The first match in the first round of the singles on the opening day, Anderson vs Woosnam, was one of those which might have gone either way. Anderson won it by

4–6, 6–2, 6–4, 6–4. The court after recent rains was playing somewhat unevenly, and under the conditions Woosnam's quickness and clever footwork stood him in good stead.

Anderson was making the finer shots, but Woosnam's sound defence caused him to 'press', and he was at times so erratic that Woosnam was on the verge of getting the upper hand. This happened in the third set, when Woosnam led by 3–1, and was within an ace of 4–2. Subsequently, with Anderson leading 4–3, Woosnam nearly won two love games in succession, and it was only by bad luck that he lost the 5–4 lead and was beaten 6–4.

In the fourth set he again led (3–0), but at this point Anderson found his best game, and thenceforward he hit with such power and precision that Woosnam could only win one more game. The third set had, in fact, proved the turning point.

Somehow, then, thanks to a string of bad luck, unfortunate timing and the sheer bad manners of his opponent commencing a run of his very best form, just when it mattered, Woosnam was well beaten. He would have been mortally embarrassed at what sounds very much like someone making a string of slightly implausible excuses on his behalf.

A match down, and British hopes were resting on the seemingly fatalistic Lowe, whose comments on the outward journey hardly matched the somewhat glowing assessment Myers had given him prior to departure. Playing against John Hawkes, a twenty-two-year-old from Geelong in Victoria, however, the Britain rose impressively to the challenge, beating him in straight sets to level the tie.

With the contest poised at a match apiece, Anderson lined up alongside Clarence Todd, a doubles player of considerable repute. Todd was to go on to play five Davis Cup matches in 1921, four of them as part of a doubles pairing, and win the lot. Of scant consolation to Woosnam and Turnbull would be that they were the only pair who managed to push him to five sets, or that they were slightly unfortunate not to put an early dent in his hundred per cent record:

There was nothing much in it for three sets, of which Woosnam and Turnbull won the first and third and were a little unlucky to lose the second at 7–9. A temporary lapse on their part then ensued – at a most inopportune time. It was mainly brought about by weak play off the ground on the part of Woosnam, and it enabled the Australian pair, who were quick to seize their advantage, to win the fourth set easily and run to 5–0 in the fifth before Woosnam and Turnbull could recover themselves. This they did to such good effect that they won the next four games. The recovery, however, had been delayed too long, and the Australians ran out on the next game.

Having seen his country through to victory over Spain at Hendon, and having safely made the long sea journey to the United States, Woosnam was now finding himself in uncharted territory – that of the loser. As unlucky as British observers might have felt them to be, the pair had fallen to the Australians in five sets. With two singles matches remaining, he and Lowe had to win both if the trip were not to turn into a time-consuming and expensive failure. Against all the odds *Lawn Tennis and Badminton* suddenly became optimistic:

> The loss of [the doubles] match was serious, but still the British position was by no means hopeless. Inasmuch as Woosnam had got within measurable distance of beating Anderson, there was a possibility that Lowe quite get there, whilst Woosnam appeared to have at least an even-money chance of beating Hawkes.

There was considerable motivation, above and beyond the usual incentives, for wanting to believe that the tie could still be salvaged. The winners knew that they would go on to meet the Danes, who had ghosted through to the semi-final, making either Britain or Australia odds-on to reach the final, where they would challenge either Japan or India for the right to take on the Americans. For Britain to progress, Lowe had to emerge victorious when he challenged Anderson. Unfortunately Lowe lost his form just as the press rediscovered their acerbic side. 'The British goose was soon cooked, for Anderson beat Lowe much more easily than he had beaten Woosnam, mainly because he was playing a good bit better.'

In other circumstances, it would be easy to conclude that Woosnam's response to the defeat was evidence that he played better when the result no longer mattered – that he found it difficult to handle the pressure in the really big matches. His sporting CV makes a nonsense of that proposition, and so it is probably more accurate to view his performance as being typical of a man who loved to compete at everything he did, regardless of the reward: 'It was nonetheless fought to a finish with commendable keenness by both men, and the majority of the onlookers stayed to see it out. Woosnam won in the end by a judicious blend of enterprise and wearing-down tactics by three sets to two.'

If the match scarcely mattered to the overall result, it remains notable, if for no other reason than it was the last singles contest Woosnam played in the competition, his subsequent involvement being limited to doubles. As such, the five-set victory he claimed, if hot and tiring in the late afternoon Pittsburgh sun, was a fitting way to take his leave.

The general feeling was that the British side had put up a reasonably strong showing, and that had some of their unavailable players been present, they might well have been too strong for the Australians. As it was, they had been far from disgraced, and the nature of the draw had conspired to see them eliminated at a much earlier stage than their abilities merited. The Australians went through to play the Danes in Cleveland, storming through 5–0, setting up a meeting with the impressively strong Japanese in the final, who had overcome the Indians by the same, comprehensive margin.

The old order looked to be seriously challenged, as the Japanese thundered past the Australians 4–1, losing only the doubles rubber in the process, but the normal run of things was swiftly re-established. The Japanese were hopeful of causing a similar upset against the waiting Americans, but their dreams were crushed, as a 5–0 victory for the United States saw the cup retained with a minimum of fuss.

♈   ♈   ♈

For the British, the competitive tennis was over and they had time to kill. The return tickets on the *Baltic* were booked for the start of September, and now, inside the first week of August, their Davis Cup was over. Woosnam filled some of the time playing golf, accepting invitations from various influential and powerful men, who had heard the British captain was something of an all-round sportsman.

A series of matches was arranged, initially purely social, but as he proceeded to win by ever-larger margins so the opposition was beefed up, as first-rate college players were produced to challenge Woosnam. He had played little since leaving Winchester, just keeping his eye in with the occasional social round during the summer – of itself evidence of the latitude Edith allowed him, given their young family and the hectic schedule he already followed. He played six matches in all, across a variety of country club courses, and, with a glorious predictability, he won each and every one.

Woosnam had very much caught the imagination of the American public, and his sporting prowess combined with British reserve was proving to be an intriguing and potent mix. His relaxed demeanour and his personable manner attracted their interest, although not to the same degree, as this exuberant excerpt from *American Lawn Tennis* magazine suggests, as his laugh did:

> I first heard Woosnam laugh at Queen's. To hear that laugh then, as now, was to hear the music of silver bells, or, to adopt Stevenson, when Max Woosnam came into the pavilion on a dark day, it was like drawing up a blind and admitting the sun.

If this was slightly gushing, almost theatrical praise, it was to prove entirely fitting. The team needed a further diversion aside from hearing of their captain's golfing triumphs – something to entertain them for the best part of a month, and it eventually came from a rather unexpected source.

Charles Spencer Chaplin was born three years before Woosnam, in 1889, in Walworth, a small area of south-east London nestling between Peckham and the Elephant and

Castle. His parents, both music-hall entertainers, split soon after his birth, and he was left with his mother, whose mental instability led to young Charles being sent briefly to the workhouse, before being moved to Hanwell School for Orphans and Destitute Children. He became something of a child star, standing in for his mother on stage when her illness stopped her from performing, before travelling to America in 1912 with Fred Karno's Fun Factory slapstick comedy company.

He shared a room with another young performer by the name of Arthur Stanley Jefferson, who became homesick and returned to England. Chaplin stayed on, and by the time his friend returned, now using the name Stan Laurel, the fortunes of both had changed somewhat. In 1914, Chaplin worked for $150 a week at Keystone Pictures; by 1916 he had moved to the Mutual stable, for $10,000 per week and a $150,000 signing-on bonus, before joining First National in 1917 for a cool million, making him the first actor ever to earn such a sum.

In 1919 he founded the United Artists studio with Mary Pickford, Douglas Fairbanks and D.W. Griffith, making him one of the biggest names in the whole of Hollywood. It was quite a rise from the workhouse of the Walworth Road, but the effects of his early life arguably still showed through. In 1918 he had married sixteen-year-old Mildred Harris, and the couple had a son, Norman Spencer Chaplin, who tragically died when only three days old. The couple went on to divorce in November 1920, which left Chaplin, with wealth almost beyond measure, looking for entertainment in the summer of 1921, before commencing a European tour in September. The presence of the British Davis Cup team was, to Chaplin's way of thinking, an excuse for some fun.

He had always been a huge tennis fan and despite having rented a large home while married to Harris, as soon as they separated he returned to the rooms at the Los Angeles Athletic Club he had rented since becoming successful. In time he was to build a mansion of his own, complete with swimming pool and tennis court. He was not averse, it appears, to spending large amounts of money on lavishly entertaining his guests, and Woosnam and his party were no exception. As we saw in the prologue, the combination of playful sportsman and egotistical film star was not to be a long-lasting one.

It is little surprise, then, given the nature of their meeting, that when it transpired that the respective parties were sailing back to England within a couple of days of each other, they chose to journey on different boats. Chaplin travelled on the *Olympic* (quite probably muttering about tennis players the whole way, while still trying to get swimming-pool water out of his ears), and Woosnam and the rest of the team returned on the *Baltic*.

After a long summer, which despite the disappointments against Australia had still seen him collect one Wimbledon title and appear in another final, Woosnam was beginning to be tipped by tennis writers as 'one to watch' in the following year. His singles play had never, in the major championships, matched his achievements in the doubles, but things were starting to change. There was a feeling that, if he took the opportunity to concentrate on his game for longer, he might develop into a world-class singles player. Concentrating on one sport for any length of time, however, was never a trait Max Woosnam could be said to have mastered.

CHAPTER EIGHT
'OUR MAX'

Common sense might have suggested that Woosnam take a break after the Davis Cup, but it was an option he neither chose nor, given his amateur status and the need to earn a living, countenanced. When one set of team mates set off on well-earned holidays, he returned to work and become reacquainted with the set he had left behind some months earlier. Within days of landing back in Liverpool, he was training with City at Hyde Road, and little more than a week later took his place in the centre of defence as they recorded a home draw with Blackburn Rovers.

While Woosnam was away, Mangnall had pulled off another audacious coup in persuading Billy Meredith to return to City from United, to fill a player-coach role. Meredith still had enough in his legs to manage twenty-five games in the coming season, and things looked set to continue improving for the Hyde Road side. For Woosnam too, having captained his club so successfully the previous season, and having now experienced captaincy on the international stage, albeit at tennis rather than football, there was also a logical progression on the horizon.

Towards the end of October 1921, he received a telegram from the Amateur Football Association, informing him that he was selected to represent his country's amateur football team against Ireland at Leicester City's ground on 12 November, and further asking whether he would captain the side. He had already turned down the opportunity to captain the English League side against Ireland a fortnight earlier, so possibly it was the lustre which international football brought with it that swayed Crossley Brothers, but they were evidently keen for their star employee to accept the invitation.

The state of amateur football was still far from healthy, however. One of the most influential and informed footballing publications of the time was *Gamage's Association Football Annual*, and its review of the season painted a bleak picture: 'Only two Amateur International matches were played by England last season, the Continental fixtures being dropped. Both Ireland and Scotland were easily beaten. The return amateur match between Ireland and France, fixed to be played at Belfast on 17 April, was cancelled by France.'

If it was sad state to see the amateur game in such a parlous condition, it was nothing more than Woosnam had predicted when the Corinthian zeal was at its pre-war height. Isolated from the higher echelons of the game by their own ideals, Woosnam was returning to a game which was close to crisis. Given the copious detail offered by *Gamage's* about almost every other aspect of football, the scant detail about the match tells its own tale:

> Played at Leicester, on Monday, 14 November, the game being postponed from the previous Saturday on account of fog. The English team gave a satisfactory display, although a number of scoring chances were missed. The only goal of the first half came in a curious manner, Adams fisting the ball into the net from a corner well-placed by Hegan. After the change of ends, Hambleton and Binks added further goals for England, and after M'Illreavey had scored for Ireland, Hambleton scored again. Result: England, four goals; Ireland, one goal.

Two things stand out in particular from that brief, stilted paragraph. Firstly, the fact that the match was delayed to a Monday – a working day – reveals that the amateurs who played the game at that time either relied on benevolent employers, or were of independent means. Secondly, the fact that a 4–1 victory could be considered 'satisfactory', despite 'a number of scoring chances being missed', shows that the concept of English footballing pre-eminence was still unchallenged, and while the World Cup had yet to be contested, the Corinthians pondered missionary-style tours to Brazil, and the opportunities for games against other far-flung nations remained limited, the challenge was unlikely to arrive.

Back in Manchester, quite possibly because of the absence of Woosnam during pre-season training and throughout the season's first few fixtures, City were finding it difficult to maintain the momentum they had enjoyed towards the end of the previous campaign. The tension was relieved by murmurs among the crowd, spurred on in a good-natured fashion by the occasional newspaper article, questioning when their all-action centre-half might finally break his duck and appear on the score-sheet. For almost an entire season Woosnam had gone up for corners and free kicks, returning back without a goal to his name. Despite his defensive abilities, the real celebrations, it was suggested, would begin when he finally put the ball in the back of the net.

Far from being bowed down by the pressure, Woosnam himself was cheerfully aware that people were worrying about when and if his goal would happen, eventually promising his colleagues that he would take them for a meal at the Midland Hotel when and if it ever transpired.

Eventually, mid-way through November 1921, and with City already leading 4–1 against West Bromwich Albion, Woosnam struck. It appears that this momentous goal inspired one local poet (and the term is used in its very loosest fashion) to put pen to paper and compose a poem entitled 'His First Goal' and dedicated 'Our Max':

What a scene of jubilation and a round of great applause,
The spectators are delighted and you need not ask the cause,
For Max Woosnam of the 'City' who at Cambridge won
*   his Blue,*
Has at last performed the function with the goal he had in view!

The Albion were opponents at Hyde Road – the favoured
  patch,
Where 'City' since 1919 have never lost a match!
This game they won by 6 to 1, but 'City's' number 5
Was Max's special effort, and its memory will survive.

Max had obtained the precious goal we'd waited for so long,
And wholehearted acclamation was his greeting from the throng!
'Twas a tribute to a genius who has won the hearts of all,
By his splendid sporting spirit and his mast'ry of the ball;

He's an absolute first rater, and one really wonders how
Those who pick the Internationals have missed him up to now
This all-round athlete, amateur, has earned a lasting fame;
He's popular with everyone; he always plays the game.

As the goal went in, the City goalkeeper, Tom Blair, was so excited he removed his gloves, threw them into the back of his own net, and sprinted the length of the pitch to join in the celebrations. 'He's only interested in that dinner at the Midland,' one spectator was heard to comment, sarcastically.

If this marked a sudden increase in the popularity of an already much-loved footballer, it also seemed to indicate the start of a new phase in an already phenomenally successful sporting life. In January 1922 Woosnam missed only his second club game since returning from the Davis Cup, as he travelled to Swansea to captain England's amateurs against

Wales. A match, perhaps, but scarcely a contest; England triumphed 7–0, scoring six times in the second half as the Welsh wilted, leaving Woosnam, in the centre of defence, with little to do, other than look on as his side's forwards dominated.

Unsurprisingly, Woosnam came through both games unscathed, playing for City the following week. He also deserves credit for keeping a straight face when being introduced to the final English goal scorer, and owner of one of the great double-barrelled names of any age, R.J. Thorne-Thorne, of Cambridge University.

City's form was beginning to suffer at the time, slumping to just two wins in ten games, which cost them any chance of improving on the previous season's second place. Nevertheless it was clear that Woosnam was continuing to impress. At the end of February 1922, he received another telegram from the footballing authorities, this time the professional rather than amateur version, informing him that he had been selected to represent England against Wales at Anfield on 13 March. Almost inevitably, he was also asked to captain the side.

England, as with City, a professional side captained by an amateur, collected a 1–0 victory during the game, meaning Woosnam had successfully captained both his country's professional and amateur football teams. As a mark of the esteem in which he was held, *Gamage's* made him their Player of the Year for 1922–23:

No player came more into the public eye last season than Maxwell Woosnam, of Manchester City, who led England to victory against Wales at Liverpool, on 13 March 1922. Ever since the war the claims of the old Cambridge man to a place in the English eleven have been canvassed up hill and down dale, but when at last his claims were recognised in preference to those of that outstanding professional centre-half, George Wilson, of Sheffield Wednesday, quite a little controversy ranged around these rival claimants to one of the most difficult and responsible positions on the soccer field.

However, Woosnam vindicated his admirers, and in the opinion of many capable judges of the game he should have played against Scotland in the big match of the year. As it was, he was the first old boy amateur to be selected for England proper since the days of Kenneth Hunt, who had come to be regarded as the last of the Corinthian Internationals.

But this genial fair-haired giant has other claims to athletic fame than those he attained on the soccer field. He is one of the best lawn-tennis players in the country, having represented England in the Davis Cup and won the Doubles' Championship at Wimbledon.

This double international – a rare distinction – by virtue of his prowess at several other games (they all come alike to Woosnam) cannot unjustly be regarded as one of the greatest all-round athletes the world has ever seen, surpassing in some respects even the great C.B. Fry.

Personally Woosnam is a most engaging fellow, who plays every one of his games in the best possible spirit and is obviously a man that every sportsman delights to honour.

Then, on 28 April 1922 in the last home match of the season, against Newcastle, Max's charmed life turned sour. About twenty-five minutes into the match he went in for a challenge which left him with a broken right shin bone.

He had received warnings, of various sorts, that eventually his style of play was likely to injure him, but knew only one way to set about the game. The wholehearted enthusiasm which made him such a sporting success was ultimately to blame for his downfall. Centre-halves in the 1920s were large, physically imposing men, and the barge and the shoulder charge were as much a part of their armoury as anything more subtle.

In one game, shortly before the accident, Woosnam recalled, ruefully, how a referee had said to him, after a particularly abrasive passage of play, 'I don't intend to whistle you again, but if you get hurt, don't blame me.' Current accounts of the match all place the blame for the accident on the wooden fence that surrounded the pitch, but this seems to be incorrect, as Woosnam himself described: 'I went out to tackle Lowe, the Newcastle outside right, and as he was going to centre I took the ball from his toes, but the winger's swing of the foot could not be delayed, and it met my right leg.'

A City fan of the time wrote his usual diary entry following the game, and it makes fascinating reading, providing a further insight into Woosnam's nature:

> I made my usual trip to the player's entrance for autographs, and stood amongst a silent crowd of sympathisers as Max, still smiling cheerfully, was carried to the ambulance on a stretcher. A small boy detached himself from the onlookers and calmly asked the injured player to sign his book. Before any of the amazed spectators could shoo the boy away, Max asked the stretcher-bearers to stop for a moment so he could sign the book.

For most of his career, Woosnam had played as many sports as he could manage, his successes silencing the purists who urged him to concentrate on just one discipline. With a single mistimed tackle, the fears they expressed so vociferously had come true. Woosnam was to miss the entire 1922 tennis season, and his daughter Penny recalls the time clearly:

> He had to sit there, in the chair in the front room, with his leg propped up and covered in bandages, and it must have been so terribly painful for him. I mean really painful, because in those days they couldn't control pain as fully as they can now, not without leaving you addicted to

morphine or something terrible like that so you just had to put up with it.

He just sat there, feeling rotten and so obviously wanting to be outside and doing something active. He never sat still, ever, and that time, when he had his broken leg, was the only time I think, apart from sometimes on Sunday mornings when he did the crossword there. I think it was a pretty tough time for everyone in the house actually, but there was nothing to be done but get on with things as best we all could.

After the excitement of the previous year, it must have been a difficult summer, not least because of the contrast. Twelve months on from landing Wimbledon titles and launching film stars into swimming pools, Woosnam was forced to sit there, in pain, waiting for a broken leg to knit back together once more.

Given his experiences of war, and his views on sport's place in the greater scheme of life – his fears of taking it all too seriously and playing without a smile on your face – it seems unlikely that Woosnam lost his sense of perspective sufficiently to become too depressed. The pain was hard to deal with, doubtless, and the frustration immense, but as Penny recalls, life had to go on. Given the way he played, the physicality of the game in the 1920s, and the uncompromising defensive style the commentators of the day all appear to have picked up on, it is not so much that Woosnam got so badly hurt that causes surprise, but that it took quite so long for it to happen. Fate had taken its time, but inevitably, it had caught up with him.

Although Woosnam sat in his chair and watched a summer pass by without being able to play a stroke, there were other distractions for him. At the end of August 1922, his son, Maxwell, was born. Maxwell's relationship with his father seems to have been a complicated one, and his attempts to chronicle his life do contain hints of a distance between them. The passage concerning his own birth is painfully understated, to the point of anonymity, with the arrival of a baby overshadowed by another – of a mechanical kind: 'After his leg was broken, soccer and tennis temporarily halted, a son was born in August 1922 and with his insurance claim money he had bought a much prized motorcycle and sidecar.'

Woosnam's recuperation eventually claimed not just the whole of the summer immediately following the injury, as everyone knew it would, but the whole of the following winter. Effectively, so everyone feared, Max Woosnam's competitive days, at least as far as football was concerned, were over.

♛   ♛   ♛

In the same way that Crossley Brothers had been keen to trade off the fame of their sporting employee, so other businesses would start to see the benefits too. The former American Davis Cup team captain Norris Williams worked at the time for the Dupont chemical firm, and was well aware of the effect a personality like Woosnam, with his social and sporting skills, could have on the business world.

Dupont had recently signed an agreement with a Cheshire-based firm called Brunner Mond, who in time would go on to merge with Nobel Explosives to become Imperial Chemical Industries, or ICI as the world now knows them. Woosnam was headhunted – successfully – from Crossleys, and became Brunner Mond's first Personnel Manager. If he could sort out disputes on the pitch between people of many and varied backgrounds, he should be able to do it in the workplace. That was the logic, and history suggests that, despite one famous hiccup, it worked very well.

While never taking a penny from his sporting achieve-ments, Woosnam was, by necessity, walking a fine line between amateurism and professionalism. His role at Crossley's had been as much about showing off his sporting talents as anything else, and he found himself at Brunner Mond as a direct result of a sporting acquaintance.

It is hard to believe that he would have chosen to live such a life for any reason other than commitment to the ideal. He had no spare time, no time for his family, for holidays or to stop and consider his achievements. He was just making one long dash through life, stitching together a tapestry of moments of greatness into one vast triumph. Occasionally, he would receive some assistance from those who admired either his stance or his talent, but as Penny recalls, the gestures of support from the family, in particular, did not go down as well as they might have:

> We would get these terribly exciting parcels from my father's uncle Hylton, who had done terribly well and had a bit of money to spend. His daughters would go to great balls and parties, and they'd send their dresses on to us when they were finished with them, which to us, as young girls, was tremendously exciting, but my mother hated it, absolutely hated it.
>
> It was just the way she was . . . she hated the idea that anyone might be looking down on us thinking we needed things. I don't think they were looking down for one minute, but that's the way she saw it and there was no way of convincing her otherwise.

An international footballer, Olympic gold medallist and Wimbledon champion, and Woosnam found himself receiving handouts from a wealthy uncle, to help make ends meet, and to allow his family a little luxury they would not otherwise have been able to afford. Woosnam's rewards never came remotely close to matching his achievements.

As the summer of 1923 came round once more, his leg had recovered enough to allow a tentative return to action on the tennis court, competing in the Northern Championships in Manchester at the start of June. He was narrowly beaten in the final of the singles by J.D.P. Wheatley, where perhaps his lack of both sharpness and fitness put paid to his chances:

> The final was brimful of thrills throughout the whole of the five sets. Wheatley won the first and third sets, and forging ahead to 5–0, looked to have the set and match in hand when Woosnam made a gallant rally and took five games off the reel. After a fine struggle Woosnam won the set at 11–9. In the fifth set Woosnam appeared to have shot his bolt; Wheatley made no mistake and won the set and match at 6–2.

The mixed doubles saw him paired with Elizabeth Ryan, and the manner in which they took the title impressed the journalists who witnessed it, who were once again in love with Woosnam, after some negative press in the run-up to the Davis Cup: 'With her new partner, Max Woosnam, Miss Ryan made a great combination; they fell into each other's stride at once. It should turn out one of the strongest pairings we have seen for some time – two up at net most of the time.'

Similarly, his performance in the men's doubles, where he won alongside Leslie Godfree, was taken as evidence that he was returning to his best form, even after missing the whole of the previous season.

Having returned from such a serious injury, and having launched such a promising start to his competitive recovery, Woosnam should have been in optimistic mood, but if he harboured any major ambitions he was keeping them close to his chest. It would certainly fit with his character, as a man who wore his talents quietly; it might equally have been the case that Woosnam knew his injury had affected his tennis more seriously than the casual observer might have noticed. While, if he was brave enough, he might still have a first-class future in football, as far as tennis was concerned, things were still very much out of his control.

Tennis in the 1920s, particularly on grass, required a lightness of foot that a once-broken leg made almost impossible. Woosnam had based his tennis career on his athletic style of play – coming to the net and chasing endlessly, refusing to accept a cause was lost. The key to his success was not so much his shot-making but his shot-saving, and with this diminished, it was inevitable that the standard of his play would suffer.

By the time the 1923 Wimbledon championships began, he was also faced with the problem of finding doubles partners of sufficient quality to form a competitive pairing. Since he had been out of the game for a year, the majority of the better exponents of doubles, particularly in the men's event, were already spoken for, leaving Woosnam to play with Donald Greig – a partnership which offered little hope of a glorious bid for the title.

An easy enough opening round saw them sweep past Horace Lester and Norman Latchford, but the draw sealed their fate in the next, matching them against Woosnam's partner of two years earlier, Randolph Lycett, and his partner from the Northern Championships, Leslie Godfree. Having won the opening set, Woosnam and Greig were soon swamped, dispatched in four sets.

In the mixed event he was partnered with Phyllis Covell, formerly Howkins, with whom he had been defeated in the final two years earlier. This time their journey through the draw was to be a much shorter one. Two straightforward victories in the opening rounds left them unprepared for the challenge of John Hillyard and Phyllis Satterthwaite, who disposed of them in straight sets with a minimum of fuss.

So often at Wimbledon and other, smaller tournaments, the doubles had been where Woosnam had shone, making up for a historical failure in singles events which persisted throughout his career. It was as if an event which did not have some kind of 'team' aspect to it somehow failed to capture his imagination, but, for the only time in his career, the Wimbledon of 1923 saw him gain more success in singles than in doubles. The first round saw a straight-sets win over Harold Price, while the second was an impressive four-set win over the very talented Englishman Theodore Mavrogordato. Impressive wins over Hillyard, who had helped knock him out of the mixed doubles, and another Englishman, Henry Mayes, led him to a quarter-final against the South African, Brian Norton:

Woosnam led Norton by 3–0 and 5–3 in the first set by crowding the net as they say in America, and would have won it if Norton had not been lobbing particularly well; but in the next two Norton still using his lobs cleverly in pursuance of the maxim that the best way to defeat a volleyer is by volleying all you can, went up himself more often than Woosnam, and so won them both fairly easily.

The defeat drove home a fact that Woosnam had been trying to ignore since he first broke his leg. He had never enjoyed the success he might have done in singles, and if his mobility decreased, even slightly, this was never going to change. He was not the only person to reach this conclusion, even if the following analysis, published in *Lawn Tennis and Badminton* in April 1923, seems a little harsh, given his achievements across the board:

Max Woosnam is a splendid, all-round athlete who has just failed to achieve the highest distinctions. His footwork is excellent – a sound player possessing most of the strokes; but none of them quite carry the modern quota of high explosive behind them. He is rather liable to be heavy about the court and his anticipation of an opponent's reply is not quite keen enough.

Possibly, and I fancy this might supply the answer, Woosnam is such a fine fellow at other games, so much sought after, that he has never been able to give the requisite time to become pre-eminent on the lawn tennis court. Three or four months a year of grass-court play nowadays won't do — the competition from the all-the-year-rounders is too intensive. It is not for me to say in this journal that I might possibly think Woosnam may have chosen the happier path through his athletic years.

It is an interesting view for two reasons. Firstly, the mention of his lack of mobility is in stark contrast to earlier reports of his abilities, and perhaps reveals just how reduced his movement around the court had been since breaking his leg. It further lays to rest a misconception about Woosnam, adopted today by almost all who speak about him, that in the 1920s he was encouraged, cheered on and celebrated for being an all-round sportsman, and that his multi-faceted approach to his sporting endeavours somehow gave him favoured Corinthian status.

In truth, as the article and others before it right back to his university years show, there were plenty of people in the 1920s who, while applauding his multitudinous talent as results forced them to, were ready to criticise him for failing to commit to one sport above others. In doing so they were forced to make some fairly harsh claims. Could it honestly be said that a Wimbledon champion and Olympic gold medallist has ever 'just failed to achieve the highest distinctions'?

And yet while the asides and the suggestions that he had somehow under-performed now seem in equal parts acerbic and absurd, the events of the following football season told a sad story about the state of Woosnam's fitness. Having not played for City for an entire season, he trained hard and was ready to lead them through the 1923–24 campaign, hoping to turn back the clock and bring them the triumph they had so narrowly missed out on two seasons earlier.

His time away from the side had seen all sorts of changes, not just among the players. The old Hyde Road ground, with its cinder slopes and cramped condition, was now a thing of the past, as the end of the lease saw it required for tramway improvements. Permission was granted for a stadium to be built in Moss Side, on the site of an old brickworks, and for a fee of £5,500, City claimed the sixteen-acre site as their own. A Manchester architect, Charles Swain, was given the job of designing the finest ground in the North, and set about the task with a degree of imagination.

Four tunnels would lead spectators into the new stadium, one from each corner, leading up from ground level so that fans could see where they were going before they actually reached the areas of terracing. Despite holding 90,000 fans, even when full the stadium would allow everyone an unimpeded view. Costing a little more than £100,000, Maine Road was a stadium of which to be proud.

Sheffield United provided their first League opposition at the new ground, on 25 August 1923, as Woosnam led the City players on to the pitch, blinking at the crowd, estimated to be in excess of sixty thousand, as a brass band played 'Ours Is a Nice House, Ours Is'.

The game was ceremonially started by the Lord Mayor of Manchester, Councillor W. Cundliffe, although Bolton referee J. Rowcroft, doubtless with his own display of ceremony, then stopped matters in order that City's Tom Johnson could start the game in a more traditional manner. As with all the best football stories, the day culminated in a 2–1 win for the new homeowners.

Having led his team out onto the pitch to rapturous applause from a crowd who had loved him more than any other City player of the age, Woosnam led them back to the dressing room victorious. It was to be the last time he ever set foot on the pitch in a City shirt.

The summer months recovering from injury had been hard, and he had harboured private doubts all along that he would ever again be able to play to the levels and in the way that he once had. The first game of the season had provided him with a target at which to aim, with the added emotional pull of playing at the new stadium, in front of the supporters who adored him. The game would also hammer home to him a harsh truth about the state of his fitness. The break had left him too slow for top-class tennis, and too frail for top-class football.

He spoke with Mangnall after the match, frankly and honestly. The warm words Mangnall used about his captain in years to come were no doubt as much due to the respect the two men showed each other, as for anything Woosnam had done for his manager while on the pitch, and this was not a time for sentiment. He was falling short of the exacting standards he set for himself.

Playing for the love of the game did not mean playing short of his abilities, and Woosnam knew that if he were to continue it would mean having to accept a level of performance far below that which he had previously shown. When he was first signed, he opted to spend time in the reserves, choosing to play in the first team only when he was fully fit to do so, and now, at the tail end of his career, his belief that only the best was good enough remained undimmed. The 'famous amateur' never showed a level of professional detachment as clearly as he did in making his decision to retire, and Mangnall knew better than to try and dissuade him.

He had played ninety-six times for City, eventually scored four goals, and claimed a place in the hearts of the fans which endures to this day. Just around the corner from Maine Road, itself now replaced by a newer stadium in the same way as it once usurped Hyde Road, is a small street. Max Woosnam Walk probably means little to most of the people who pass along it each day, but as a quiet reminder of the deeds of a local hero, its name is hard to beat.

It was time for a break – time to sit back, look at an unparalleled career, and relax, allow himself to appreciate that which he had spent the last few years tearing round too quickly to register. He was an amateur, though, and as such a break and the time to reflect would never arrive. Just as holidays were virtually non-existent during the course of his career, so there was little opportunity to take one at its end.

The remainder of the winter was spent working, which admittedly involved a combination of factory floor and golf course, while keeping a keen eye out for the progress of City. It was not just his football that had fallen from the level Woosnam felt it had once been. In his own mind, and evidently that of the Davis Cup selectors, with his singles days behind him Woosnam was now a doubles specialist only. At the start of May 1924, he was selected for the team to play Belgium in the first-round tie at Torquay, but only in the doubles alongside Godfree. It was to prove a successful combination. Belgium were defeated by three rubbers to two, with Woosnam and Godfree coming victoriously through their match against Jean Washer and Georges Watson in straight sets.

For Woosnam and his colleagues, the decision to play the next round at Edgbaston was an important one. On a clay surface the Spanish side were developing into a world-class side, but on the faster, grass courts of Edgbaston, it was a different matter. In Alonso they had a player of almost incomparable talent who had won both of his singles matches, against Wheatley and Gilbert, and the tie would have been lost had it not been for Woosnam and Godfree. Their partnership was looking continually more impressive, and there were calls for them to continue this pairing at Wimbledon.

Their combined skills meant a relatively smooth victory over Alonso and Eduardo Flaquer. Britain's second successive 3–2 win saw them to a European group semi-final against South Africa in Scarborough, at the start of June 1924. Woosnam was still very well received by the British tennis-watching public, and the crowds had always retained a soft spot for him, but he was having to dig deeper than ever before to achieve the levels he had once set for himself.

Britain claimed all four singles matches against the South Africans, to take the tie with a minimum of difficulty, but in the doubles Godfree and Woosnam were beaten, 11–9, 7–5, 6–4. Sadly, it marked the beginning of the end for Woosnam, at least as far as the international stage was concerned:

> Woosnam today was lobbable; he was uncertain in returning a fast service ball. In both respects he has ever been thus. But where he generally scores is in the fast, back-chat play at the net. Today, he often was beaten in that department. It would be quite unjust to leave the impression that Woosnam was really bad. He did many bright and clever things. He was the type of player whom I personally would like better than any other to see as Britain's first string in both singles and doubles. But as now he isn't – so I cannot pretend. Sadly, the weakest man of today's foursome was Woosnam.

The win had brought Britain through to a tie against France, to be played at Eastbourne in the last week of July, but doubts must have been circulating in Woosnam's mind as to how much longer he could continue to compete at this level. The French provided a large part of the answer, easily winning the tie 4–1, while the dazzling pairing of Jean Borotra and Jacques Brugnon comfortably claimed the doubles rubber. Having previously lavished rapturous reports on his sporting career, the journalists had been slower to applaud and swifter to criticise in the previous twelve months. This summary of his part in the French match was another example of damning with faint praise – 'Woosnam's backhand return of service always offered a wide target, yet both he and Godfree played well through the second set.'

His talents on the tennis court had started to fade, and being more acutely aware of the fact than anyone else, Woosnam prepared to take a step back from sport. His injury left his abilities diminished, and pride dictated he rebalance his life towards work, rather than play. He had played his last Davis Cup match, and that year's Wimbledon, he decided, would also be his last.

His farewell performance in the men's doubles, the event at which he had been champion, was in partnership with John Wheatley, a sometime Davis Cup player, but never a sufficiently strong partner to challenge for the title. After three early victories against opposition who failed to generate so much as a footnote in the history books, they met Francis

Hunter and Vincent Richards in the quarter-final. Having lost the first two sets, they claimed the third to threaten a comeback, but succumbed immediately, losing 2–6, 5–7, 6–3, 4–6.

In the mixed doubles, he was partnered for one last time by Phyllis Covell, and again he swept through a trio of opening matches, before being drawn against two of the biggest names in the game, his old favoured opponent, Suzanne Lenglen, and her partner Borotra, in the quarter-final. Even had he been defeated, it would have been difficult to argue that such a match would not have left Woosnam's mixed doubles career on the high point it deserved.

Sadly, however, Lenglen was forced to withdraw from the tournament as a result of an asthmatic problem, and the match was conceded as a walkover. It left a semi-final against Leslie Godfree, his Davis Cup partner, and Dorothy Shepherd Barron, which, despite his opponents losing the opening set and then levelling at one apiece, saw Woosnam and Covell succumb 4–6, 6–4, 4–6.

His singles play at Wimbledon had never been overly impressive, so it was perhaps ironic that he ended his career against one of the greats of that, or any other age – Borotra, the 'Bounding Basque'; and as with his final Davis Cup appearance, he lost the opening two sets, claimed one back, and then fell at the next, eventually losing 3–6, 5–7, 6–2, 4–6.

The Wimbledon crowd loved him as much as ever, and

his smile and general good humour provided a genuine feel-good factor around the tournament, but inside he was fighting the feelings any human being would have experienced at the end of such a glorious chapter of his life. Sport did not so much define him as make up a part of him, but to the outside world it was a different matter. A sporting force of nature had faded and dimmed, and nobody could fail to feel some sadness at its passing.

Woosnam had chosen a suitably prestigious opponent against whom to take a final Wimbledon bow, but in realistic terms, the tournament had offered no reason for him to review his decision to take a step away from the competitive game and into the shadows. He had never been an extraordinary shot-maker, or a player blessed with incredible touch. In much the same way he excelled as a footballer, he was a man who used the core components of his athletic ability to their limits.

Despite his barrel-chested physique and a reputation for fearsomeness, he was a quick and agile, nimble and gymnastic man, and the praise offered to him throughout his career reflected that – 'Woosnam's ability to return shots others would have left for dead', and 'the bounding and bouncing figure of Woosnam'. Now, with an injury robbing him of such attributes, he knew it was time to walk away from competitive sport.

The same search for perfection that influenced the decision which launched his career would end it. He would continue to play tennis on a social basis, but as far as the highest level was concerned, aged thirty-three, Max Woosnam had taken his final bow.

CHAPTER NINE

A BLOT ON THE COPYBOOK

Although Woosnam had made his decision and walked away, competitive sport seemed unwilling to recognise the end of their relationship, and during the first few years of his retirement the newspapers continued to feature heartfelt tributes. Among the first to appear were the memories of Mangnall, his manager at Manchester City, whose recollections appeared under the headline 'Greatness of Woosnam – Stories from the Career of a Personality' in the *Empire News* of 8 March 1925. If Woosnam had been hoping to slip off anonymously, Mangnall's praise was not going to make things any easier:

> I approach the career of my esteemed friend with the utmost diffidence because I know how he dislikes eulogies of himself, and because I am conscious of how easy it is to appear a flatterer when using adjectives to describe a man which, when used to their fullest, can do no more than justice merits and demands.

In July of 1921 he was selected as captain of the British Davis Cup lawn tennis team, and he sailed for America. Replying to a congratulations telegram I sent to him, he said he would let me know directly he got back in case we were still short of a centre-half for the reserves. That observation was typical of Max. All that mattered to him was getting the chance to play the game he so dearly loved. It proved what a genuine sportsman he was. He has left behind him a name that will remain fresh for many years with the club and among football enthusiasts generally – a great sportsman, and an English gentleman with the most charming personality.

Sadly the accolades were soon to turn to anger and hostility but it was business, not sport, that caused the ructions. Having been offered a position with Brunner Mond which could have been, and in truth probably was, created with him in mind, Woosnam's attitude to life, and the pace at which he continued to live, did not change noticeably in the months which followed his sporting 'retirement'. For the first time in his life, he was genuinely capable of making his sporting activities fit around his work, in place of the compromised arrangements he had been forced to adopt while at Crossley Brothers.

Woosnam's determination to throw himself into a business career which hitherto had taken a back seat was genuine. Occasionally, this determination meant he acted with rather more gusto than was wise, be it an over-zealous shoulder barge on the football pitch, or his rash treatment of Charlie Chaplin. Neither caused long-term damage, but the day arrived when his values would cause problems which were more difficult to smooth over.

It came in the early days of May 1926, shortly after his retirement, as the General Strike gripped the country. Britain had been heading towards an economic crisis for some years; coal stocks had been depleted during the First World War, and this, coupled with free coal being taken from Germany by way of reparations, put the mining industry in particular in a precarious position.

Mine owners responded by announcing that they would be reducing the wages of mine workers, causing the Trades Union Congress to step in and back their members. Conservative Prime Minister Stanley Baldwin entered the argument, seeing the likely consequence, and declared that the Government would provide a nine-month subsidy in order to maintain the wage structure, and hopefully avert the threat of industrial action.

The miners, prematurely, took the move as a sign of victory, but the climb-down was strategic, buying the Government nine months in which to prepare for an inevitable conflict. A Government-instigated report from the Samuel Commission emerged shortly afterwards, and recommended that wages would indeed have to be cut, that the subsidy should cease, and that the industry required a major overhaul. This eventually led mine owners to announce wages would be reduced by between 10 and 25 per cent.

In response, the TUC Conference met on 1 May 1926, and announced a general strike was to begin on 3 May. Unwilling to be seen bringing what could be construed as 'revolutionary' elements into the dispute, the TUC called upon only the workers in key areas to withdraw their labour – railways, transport workers and dockers, among others. It was an organisational disaster, as the Government relied on the reserves and planning it had put into place after buying itself time with the promise of a subsidy.

The formal strike ended on 12 May, failing even to force the Government to guarantee that there would be no victimisation of strikers. Miners continued their protest for as long as they could, but faced with horrendous poverty and a real threat of starvation they gave in, and by November the strike had been broken and the mines were working again. It was a bitter blow and a heavy defeat for the trade unions and the working man, and against the background of anger and hardship, feelings ran understandably high.

Brunner Mond tried to keep production progressing as best it could, despite lacking the transport workers it needed to move its chemical supplies around. With nobody to drive a bus for the firm, Woosnam stepped behind the wheel, either not thinking or not caring about the longer-term consequences, and drove it himself. In his ongoing determination to get things done the working-class hero had become a strike breaker.

His popularity in Manchester was affected, as the heavily industrialised area in which he lived felt the bite of the Government backlash more acutely than most. As enraged as the Brunner Mond workforce must have been, however, it was the Manchester City fans who took his actions most keenly to heart. In such a time of hardship and poverty, heroes were important – heroes gave people who were hungry and scared someone to look up to. The system could deny you money, food, warmth, security and a hundred other things, but heroes were beyond its reach. Heroes sat alongside dreams and hopes, enabling the bleakest moment to look brighter, with precious moments of escapism. When Woosnam appeared to show that he cared nothing for the ordinary people of Manchester, their anger and upset was both understandable and inevitable.

As his son remembered, a policeman was deputed to patrol the grounds of Hollybank, the house in Altrincham where he lived with his young family, although the protests, while furious, were peaceful. Stripped of their livelihoods, the unemployed workers were determined to retain their dignity, even if they could not retain their jobs. For Woosnam, it was a difficult time. He still had all the home comforts he had worked for, and was suffering none of the financial hardship some of his former employees were enduring. He also knew he had forfeited both their affection and their respect. A sporting career gilded by talk of him being a man of the people had survived little more than two years of retirement before the tarnish appeared.

Woosnam was not alone in his actions – many in London were doing much the same thing – but his relationship with the working man, forged through seasons of support from the terraces, made his decision harder to explain. His politics always remained a personal matter, never discussed in public, even if his attitudes and expressions give a distinct hint of social conservatism. If sport had allowed him to cross boundaries of class, the strike saw him, in the eyes of many, forced to nail his colours to the mast.

It is too easy to take aim at Woosnam and paint him as an arrogant man, breaking the strike without a care and troubling himself even less over the consequences. Penny Kavanagh attempts to put his actions into context:

It was drilled into us that you had a duty to do what you could, to make sure that if you could help, you would. I moved back to England ten years ago, and before that I was in Ireland. There was an RNLI fundraising group, to raise money for the lifeboats, and I went along, and eventually they asked who would help organise things for the next year, because they had an annual fete which needed arranging. Nobody else put their hand up, so I saw it as my duty to do something, and ended up with the job.

I had been taught, as I say, that if you could help someone, you should.

Well, the year after I started, it made £25,000 on the day, and it had made £1,500 the year before, so that was a bit of an improvement. You can say what you like, you see, and moan about the state of things, but you need to just get stuck in sometimes and do whatever you can to help other people when you can. It's a Woosnam trait, the Woosnam way, and it took someone to stand up and jolly well get things done. Hard work and dedication – there's nothing magic about it, just hard work and a refusal to be beaten.

The episode during the General Strike was very similar to that. He just believed that things should get done, regardless of the circumstances.

However, Max Woosnam certainly hadn't remained isolated in his own corner of the country, unaware of what happened elsewhere and was well acquainted with of the 'bigger picture'. Indeed, in those days of restricted foreign travel, his sporting journeys to Europe, Brazil, the United States and elsewhere, coupled with his education and business experience, gave him a better and wider perspective on the problems in hand than many others could have possibly aspired to.

The war was still fresh in the memories of the population, and the hardship and poverty they faced left tensions stretched to their limits. Woosnam appears to have been progressing through the firm well, and his promotion to Welfare and Employment Manager suggested some degree of insight on his part into the conditions faced by the other employees. His working career would continue along similar lines, directly related to understanding the emotions and the feelings of the workers, and liaising between them and the management of the firm.

Whether or not he felt that jumping in a bus in order that things 'should get done' was defensible on a personal level, it is hard to imagine that he would not have realised how provocative his actions were, had he stopped to think. Yet he was not an arrogant man, and had spent a sporting career making sure that nobody could possibly level such an allegation at him. Woosnam had not constructed his much-loved character simply because he was aware of its personal benefits later in life. On the face of it, he was a well-balanced, intelligent man, respectful of the feelings of others, and widely praised by those who met him for exactly those traits. He certainly understood all too well the importance of playing as a team. Despite his Cambridge education and international success, he was never superior or unapproachable in manner and the fact that a team of hardened professional footballers had approached their manager and asked that he be made their captain attested to that.

Perhaps the most likely explanation is simply that Woosnam took his duty to his employer very seriously.

Throughout his life, from Cambridge days onwards, he had found himself trapped between the expectations of the public and the reality of life as an amateur. At first glance it appeared to be one long trail of glory, but the reality of amateurism was that all the glory in the world didn't pay the rent. Whether it be the presents from his uncle Hylton or the orders of Crossley Brothers that he play for Manchester City, Woosnam had long been aware that behind the acclaim for his sporting prowess, he had to rely on the largesse of others to allow him to compete at all. At the time of the strike, Woosnam had been at the firm for only a few years, and would have been well aware that he owed his job to Norris Williams, the American who offered it to him having met him through the Davis Cup.

Woosnam had a young family, had just reached the end of one career, and knew that for the sake of that family his new one had to be a success. On top of that was a question of loyalty. Was his primary loyalty to the men who worked with him, or the man who had given him the job? In all likelihood, he was partly ignoring the seriousness of his actions when he decided to drive the bus that day, so that he might bring an immediate solution to an immediate problem. Perhaps, deeper down and with a heavy heart, he had known what it would do to the people who had respected and revered him. He had been strangled by his own code of personal conduct, which told him that he was in debt to his employers. The very amateurism for which people loved him eventually led him to make a decision that, for a while, made them hate him just as powerfully. More than that we will never know, but the actions of an instant had damaged a reputation garnered over a lifetime. Thousands of others, in far more precarious financial situations than Woosnam's chose to support the strike, and he did not.

♔   ♔   ♔

His career went on to flourish, and the backlash, while bitter, was not permanent. In 1934 he became, along with his role at ICI, a director of North East Marine, a company run by Mr O.J. Philipson, the son of Woosnam's uncle Hylton, who, before Woosnam's talents became fully apparent, had been the sporting hero of the family. The firm went on to merge with the Richardsons, Westgarth Group, and he duly became a director of the newly formed company, proving that his ability to be in the right place at the right time extended beyond the sporting arena and into the boardroom. But it was his talents and hard work that ensured he remained a well-regarded and successful figure for the rest of his career.

As a Richardsons, Westgarth newsletter explained, in an article about Woosnam shortly before his retirement:

> His contribution to the Group's affairs goes far beyond the field of personnel matters. Somehow things go better when he is present, with his apt comments founded on keen observation and a quick intellect.

In all kinds of places one encounters the esteem in which he is held amongst those who knew sport in the twenties. When a few weeks ago, shortly after one of his frequent trips to Tyneside, one of his fellow Directors was having a haircut at the Station Hotel, Newcastle, the barber remarked with uninhibited enthusiasm, 'That was a very fine gentleman you were with in the hotel the other day, Sir. Mr Woosnam was always one of my heroes when I was a boy. I could always get more for a swap of one of his photos than for anyone else's.'

Despite this new commitment to work, Woosnam didn't give up sport altogether. He continued to play tennis at club and county level for many years and occasionally played football for Northwich Victoria in the Cheshire County League. Manchester City also retained a huge affection for Woosnam. After his retirement, he was often invited to the ground to watch games, and when they won the FA Cup in 1934 he went to the banquet which followed, where Sam Cowan, the City captain, introduced Woosnam to his wife as 'the greatest centre-half and captain Manchester City ever had'.

Even in retirement and well into his forties, his presence appears to have inspired and intrigued competitors and spectators alike, just as much as it ever had. The point is underlined by an article by Stanley Doust, which appeared in the *Daily Mail* in August 1933. Then, as now, the hysteria of middle England was always likely to raise a smile elsewhere:

Bad manners on and off the lawn-tennis court of some of our well-known players was the subject of a letter I received from a spectator who is a friend of mine. My friend accuses one player of constant abuse of his partner in a voice sufficiently loud to be heard by spectators and behaviour generally for which any boy at a decent public school would be soundly beaten.

My friend goes on to say that these people were not lacking good example, as Woosnam and Lester notably not only played better than any of them, but showed how a game should be played. Unless the game is rigidly controlled, we shall not escape unpleasant incidents which are un-British and thoroughly abominable. I know the LTA are primarily responsible, but I regard them as an effete body.

Quite whether the fears of Mr Doust's friend about the effeminacy of the tennis authorities were justified or not is hard to say at this distance. Equally, the question of whether the looming threat of a sound beating best ensures correct behaviour on the tennis court is hard to judge, although the prospect of the tournament referee announcing, Basil Fawlty-style, that Mr McEnroe was going to get a 'damn good thrashing' has a certain comic attraction.

For all the achievements he garnered while on the court, to Woosnam, the prospect of being remembered as a man who played the game in the right spirit and for the right reasons was, perhaps, the most pleasing.

This new phase in his life also allowed Woosnam the opportunity to discover new sports and again prove his multifarious talents. He played snooker on an occasional basis, and purely socially, while active as a footballer and tennis player, but when his role in those games became itself more social, he began to take to the green baize more seriously. Evidently intrigued by a new challenge, he played with work colleagues more and more frequently, fuelling further absences from what his son politely described as the 'humdrum necessities of life'.

His natural ball skills, hand–eye coordination and flair for anything sporting immediately showed themselves in this new discipline, however, and within a couple of years of taking up the game seriously he notched several century breaks and eventually, it is recorded, a maximum 147 break. It was, in hindsight, a good thing that he was such lively and compelling company, because with his habit of being particularly good at absolutely everything at which he tried his hand, he would surely otherwise have been unbearable.

One further sporting triumph, if indeed it can be described as such, came about in 1929, and it would be wrong to chronicle Maxwell Woosnam's achievements without paying tribute to his final doubles triumph. The name of his partner has been lost to history, but October 1929 saw him gain second place in the hotly contested budgerigar section of the Wirral and District Cage Bird Annual Show.

Many of the moments in Woosnam's life raise a smile, several a brief moment of amazement, but the common thread remains the inability to predict quite what he was going to do next. With the help of a small bundle of coloured feathers with a high-pitched squeak, and the good taste of the Wirral and District judges, Woosnam ensured the unexpected twists and turns of his career continued; just as people felt it safe to assume that his competitive days were over, he added one more accolade to his Olympic triumph, his Wimbledon title and his international caps.

No story like Woosnam's would be complete without a red herring thrown in somewhere. Such were the diversity of his achievements, it was inevitable that a few fanciful suggestions as to his claims to fame should have appeared. There was, a little over a decade ago, a highly plausible suggestion that he was a fine small-bore rifle shot, and had appeared at Bisley in 1925. Strictly speaking, this may of course be true, but of the multitude of episodes detailed here, it is the only fact about Woosnam which cannot be verified. As Ted Molyneux, the Honorary Curator of the National Rifle Association museum, observes:

> Unfortunately our records contain no mention of Max Woosnam at all, although he may have shot in some military competitions of which we have no records. It would seem though, that the sports at which he excelled are not conducive to good target shooting!

If his children had ever hoped that the end of his sporting career would bring about opportunities to see more of their father, however, they appear to have been mistaken. His son noted:

> In addition to the county tennis championships, sport took him away from his home life with great frequency, as golf, snooker, squash and social games of tennis occupied every out of office moment.
>
> Wives know only too well that one top class sport can widow them at an early age. Max's wife, with three children, could tell them what four first class sports could mean. It is difficult enough to criticise when outstanding people in any sphere, faced with the choice of doing something they are blessed with being able to do exceptionally well, are in conflict with the more humdrum necessities of life. Creative talent is uncommon enough to justify special measures but there is a sacrifice to be paid somewhere, as every famous person knows.

Through his own determination to make the best of both worlds, and by 'burning the candle at both ends', Woosnam managed to ensure that his business affairs progressed much more efficiently than they might otherwise have done. The net result was a family who rarely saw their father. In the 1920s and 1930s, the idea of being a hands-on father was beyond the comprehension of all but a very few, and it had never been something which was expected or required of Woosnam, as Penny, recalls.

> That was just the way it was, and you weren't invited to
> have an opinion or at least to offer it forwards. The men
> went out and did the paid work, while the women stayed
> at home and did the domestic work, whatever that work
> may have been. With his sporting activities as well, no, I
> didn't see as much of my father as a child might these days,
> but that was just the way life was. My father might have
> been away more than most, but we certainly weren't
> unique.

Perhaps it is a sign of the age in which Woosnam's children
were brought up, maybe it is simply evidence of the *way* in
which they were brought up, but chiselling out much more
than the factual details of family life from Penny is difficult.
Their generation's roles were set out along deeply traditional
lines, the work ethic and desire to see things through
imprinted onto the minds of all of them. There were no short
cuts, and while nothing guaranteed success, nothing made it
so likely as hard work. From these traditional, ordinary
ground rules came extraordinary people.

The era that instilled Woosnam's modesty and determination also encouraged his reserve and a certain emotional
shyness. Himself at boarding school from such a young age,
Max Woosnam may well have found it hard to react to his
own children. While his son's memories are recorded with
awe and admiration, they lack warmth. As he reflected

several years ago, in a very rare interview with the *Mail on Sunday*:

> He encouraged me to take up tennis but he never found time to coach me. The sad truth is that I never really knew him. In those days you were sent off to boarding school because they didn't trust mothers to look after you. Then it was Winchester, then Cambridge; I never really saw him.
>
> I scarcely ever had a conversation with him. I do remember playing tennis with him in 1949, when he was 57. He beat me. When he moved down to London I should have said, come on let's have lunch once a week. But I never did.

And yet, while he may find warmth hard to come by, there is no doubting the immense pride with which Maxwell Jnr reflected on his father's achievements. At the bottom of four pages of closely typed memories, it is signed, with a signature remarkably similar to the one his father had used at Winchester almost seventy-five years earlier. Beneath the signature, his name is typed out 'Maxwell S Woosnam (son)' and dated 'April 1987, Malmesbury'.

It is that single word, contained within brackets at the end of his name, which tells you a little of the pride the writer feels, and perhaps something of the regret he bears at getting closer to the man through the recording of his achievements than he did throughout the course of his life. To read the whole line suddenly provokes unexpected feeling. Its accuracy is matched only by its poignancy, as it brings to an end a document which stirs all manner of disquieting emotions. There was certainly love between father and son, although perhaps not of a kind that could be considered effusive or colourful. Instead, a son, trying to summarise his father for the benefit of a wider audience, seems strangely limited in the words he uses and the events he recalls, and instead reverts to listing the achievements of the man, rather than describing the man himself.

♔   ♔   ♔

With the outbreak of the Second World War, life changed for Woosnam, as it did for so many. Edith had been ill for some time with cancer, and within a month of the commencement of hostilities she died. Shortly after Edith's death he moved to London. He had been made the Personnel Director of the General Chemicals Division of ICI, and with his children having grown up and been called upon to join the services, there was in his mind no reason to remain in the north. And with that, a lifetime's attachment to the north-west, with only his war service and education aside, came to an end, as if Edith was the last remaining anchor keeping him there.

A year after moving with ICI to London he joined the staff of the ICI Personnel Director, acting as Personal

Assistant, before being appointed, three years later, to the position of Personnel Manager of ICI Head Office and Sales Regions. Within twenty years of ending his career as one of the greatest sportsmen of the age, he had worked his way up onto the board of ICI. Suddenly the times he spent at Winchester and Cambridge enjoying the company of people, rather than books, seemed to be paying off.

It was in London that he met and married his second wife, Dorothy. Relations between his children and their step-mother were, Penny suggests, cordial without becoming warm. It seems that having spent long periods away from his children when they were young, Wosnam did not attempt to correct the balance later in life: 'He was never really, I suppose, Max the father, as much as he was Max the sportsman, but you didn't question that because that was just the way it was, the way the world worked. It certainly didn't strike me as anything particularly extraordinary. To me, it was just how Max, how Dad, was.'

♔   ♔   ♔

While Max Woosnam is not celebrated to the extent that one would expect of a sporting figure of his prowess, he has been remembered in the sporting press on a sporadic basis, as this comment on his career in Charles Buchan's *Football Monthly* from the early 1950s shows:

On the soccer field he always reminded me of the late Charlie Roberts, whom I considered the ideal centre-half. Max had the same commanding physique, the same slight crouch on the field, and almost an equal ability in bringing the ball under control in a flash and sending it unerringly to a winger.

Woosnam played his game as if he thoroughly enjoyed every minute of it. And at the end of the hardest league game or cup tie he seemed as fresh as the most highly trained professional opponent to him. Yet he never spared himself. He covered a tremendous amount of ground with his long raking strides, but he was rarely caught out of position. In the days when centre-halves were expected to start attacks, Max had few equals.

Woosnam gave great service to both Manchester City and Chelsea. I wish there were more like him in the game today. It needs personalities of his kind.

If his relationship with family was an area of some sadness, his charm, as far as the rest of the world was concerned, evidently remained undiminished. His work colleagues seem to be able to offer nothing but a string of eulogies to the power of his personality, and his retirement in 1954 was genuinely lamented. In *ICI News*, Mr A.J. Quig, a Deputy Chairman of the company writes,

> While I know it is true, I cannot become accustomed to the fact that Max Woosnam has reached the age of

retirement. His judgement of human beings, his capacity to be gentle, yet firm and his generosity and kindliness to his colleagues amounted to qualities so important that they will be greatly missed.

His retirement from ICI did allow him more time to devote to Richardsons, Westgarth and its associated companies, however, and he spent his time touring their various sites around the country, and giving what can only be described as pep-talks. This local newspaper report from 1958 offers an insight into his style:

Hobbies are 'wonderfully good levellers' and a good way of taking away people's conceit, Mr Max Woosnam told apprentices at the North-Eastern Marine Engineering Co, Ltd, works at Wallsend yesterday.

Presenting the awards at the annual prize distribution, Mr Woosnam said it was not much good going home and turning on the wireless or television set or sitting in a cinema.

'If you put all you have into some hobby you will be successful. You will meet other people and you will achieve happiness.'

It was a theory which Penny, still echoes half a century later. If anything, the daughter manages to make the father look like something of a soft-liner:

If you've got money to drink yourself into slobbery, then

you've got enough to do something with your life, to do something more amazing than just get fat and idle. If you don't take that chance, and you just choose to let it all pass you by in a haze while you complain about your lot, then I'm sorry, but I can't see that you've much of a case for asking anyone to feel sorry for you. It was your own lack of adventure and spirit leaves you high and dry. All of us can control our lives more than we think we can, and all of us should aspire to that every single day.

As part of the same 'tour' Woosnam addressed the crowd at Maine Road, introducing young people taking part in the National Fitness display, a gloriously kitsch piece of choreographed callisthenics, featuring bare-chested young men in shorts and plimsolls leaping and bounding across the turf. Standing there in a three-piece suit, replete with handlebar moustache and microphone, Woosnam looks like the ringmaster at a particularly camp circus. Thankfully, he clearly had a sufficient stock of goodwill left with the City crowd to save him from the mockery others might have received in the same situation.

It wasn't just his own businesses that benefited from his energy and enthusiasm. He continued his involvement with tennis, playing a leading role in the affairs of the International Lawn Tennis Club of Great Britain. One of his contributions to future generations was the Cheshire County Doubles Championships, which he set up in the hope of improving the overall standard of doubles in the country, with a view to developing future Wimbledon champions. His health, however, was beginning to fade as the effects of his lifelong smoking habit – a habit then not known to be damaging – began to take their toll. His son recalled,

> He was still good looking and an outstanding figure, he played tennis and golf whenever he could, but his lungs started to cause him serious concern. An athlete who never spared his body in competition, a smoker and long hours at work and play in the shadow of a chemical factory, began to take their toll.

In other words, forty years of running around amid the fall-out from chemical smokestacks, stopping only to light another Capstan Full Strength, had left his lungs somewhat tired. The image of the dashing, cigarette-smoking sportsman he had cultivated and enjoyed during his earlier years seems, sadly, to have helped kill him.

Max Woosnam died on 14 July 1965 in a London hospital as a result of myriad respiratory problems. A remarkable life was brought to an end in pain and suffering, but few people ever died with so little to regret about how very thoroughly they had lived their life to the full.

His obituary notices appeared in publications spanning the same breadth as his achievements, including broadsheets like the *Telegraph*, *The Times* and the *Guardian*, and alongside the common ground of triumph and success they all recount, there are individual references, distinct to each of his environments, which offer a final insight into the man. It is, perhaps inevitably, Penny who best sums up what her father did, and what he represented, while accepting that he has slipped from history's gaze:

> I'm not entirely surprised he's been a bit forgotten, because he didn't really seek out the sort of headlines which would have seen him remain in people's memories. He wasn't flamboyant in the sense that he sought to gain huge attention for his achievements. He was a natural competitor and he liked people to enjoy what he did and the way he did it, but his real drive came from a sense of contentment at a job well done and a game well enjoyed, rather than because of the cheers or the acclaim of a crowd.
>
> He achieved so much more than so many modern sportsmen, without ever receiving or asking for a fraction of the praise or the attention. It would have been all too easy for him to make more of a name for himself, to seek out a place in the newspapers, but that just wasn't him, you see, just wasn't what he was all about.

Aside from all his sporting triumphs, it is the bravery he showed and the horrors he and millions of others faced on the battlefields of the First World War which tell of his character. When his extraordinary and glorious life came to an end, it was a man who understood those horrors who stood up to pay tribute.

Brigadier Sir John Smythe VC commanded men on the battlefields of the Second World War, committed acts of extraordinary bravery, and stood as a symbol of everything an active, adventurous man could hope to become. Max Woosnam was his friend and his hero. On 2 September 1965, some weeks after an understated, and underwhelming cremation in Liverpool (remembered by Penny so acutely as being 'a horrible, dismal little affair'), Smythe gave the address at Woosnam's memorial service, held at St Michael's Church, in Chester Square, Belgravia:

> Max Woosnam was one of the great all-round ball players of his time – and indeed of any other time. At any game which demanded the quick coordination of eye, foot, hand and body, he was quite outstanding, and these qualities combined with a powerful physique, brought him many successes in the world of sport.
>
> He brought a spirit of gaiety and adventure to all the games he played, and into his everyday life. Whatever game he played, or whatever else he did, he did with all his might – and he took his defeats with the same good temper and serenity as he took his victories.
>
> To say that Max Woosnam will be missed in the world of sport is an understatement. His death leaves a gap which can never be filled, and he leaves behind him a host of friends and admirers.

And sport, as the Brigadier had observed, knew that it would never see his like again – a man whose plain and understated memorial stone near his childhood home stands in such stark contrast to the colourful and successful life he led. But as Penny mused:

> How could anyone do justice to him and the things he achieved anyway? Be silly to try. Some people only get praised after they die, only get the plaudits they deserve once they're pushing up the daisies. Not my father though, not by a long chalk. He lived life like a hero, which, to a lot of people, is rather what he was. Not that he'd have ever thought it of himself. That wouldn't have been right.

ACKNOWLEDGEMENTS

There are a large number of people, without whose help, expertise and kindness this book would never have existed.

In vaguely chronological order, thanks are due to David Beach at Horris Hill, Penny McPherson at Winchester and Jacqueline Cox and Jonathan Smith at Cambridge University. I also owe a huge debt of gratitude to Joy Hamer, for her help with events surrounding Aberhafesp, and to David Whalley and Malcolm Burr for their pen portraits of Woosnam which proved very useful. Particular thanks go to Gary James at Manchester City, who went out of his way to provide information and statistics, along with Ceri Stennett from the Welsh FA, and Colin Cameron, who was as generous as ever with both his time and his footballing knowledge.

Peter Holme from the National Football Museum went repeatedly above and beyond the call of duty to drag out numerous documents and photographs, likewise John Edgar from ICI. Thanks also to Audrey Snell at the All England Club's Kenneth Ritchie library, who couldn't have been any more helpful or pleasant. I also owe a debt of gratitude to various journals, books and newspapers, including Jimmy Stow's history of Horris Hill, *Lawn Tennis and Badminton*, *The Times*, *Mail on Sunday*, *The Field*, *Manchester Guardian*, *Gammage's Football Annual*, *Burke's Sporting Who's Who*, and a host of others.

I have to thank the Woosnam family, for their kindness and assistance in helping me to tell a story as personal to them as it is exhilarating to everyone else. To Denise Patterson and Maxwell Woosnam and also to Jean and Hughie Webb, but above all perhaps, to Penny Kavanagh, who sat and talked with me, who collected together cuttings and documents, and whose calm determination to see her father's story told was an inspiration.

From Aurum Press, thanks are due to Piers Burnett, who listened and had the faith to turn the idea into a reality. Particular thanks are also due to Natasha Martin, my editor, who encouraged and advised throughout. Without her invaluable habit of forcing the matter onwards, I would doubtless have prevaricated endlessly, rather than actually getting on with writing.

On a personal level, thanks are owed to all those friends, The Far Canal, Charlie Connelly and others, without whom life would be drier and duller, and of course to my family, for a million different reasons. To my Mum and Dad, though, I owe particular thanks, Mum for her love and support and Dad for the same, as well as discovering 'Max' in the first place, many years ago. I hope I did the tale justice.

To my darling wife Cas, all my love and thanks, because as you know, I really couldn't do any of it without you. Finally, to my daughters, Honor and Amy – Daddy's finished his book, so yes, you can play on the computer now.

INDEX